*Cambridge Studies in Social Anthropology*

*General Editor: Jack Goody*

51

INDIVIDUAL AND SOCIETY IN GUIANA

*For other titles in this series turn to page 125*

# Individual and society in Guiana

## A comparative study of Amerindian social organization

PETER RIVIÈRE
*University of Oxford*

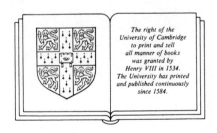

The right of the
University of Cambridge
to print and sell
all manner of books
was granted by
Henry VIII in 1534.
The University has printed
and published continuously
since 1584.

CAMBRIDGE UNIVERSITY PRESS

*Cambridge*
*London   New York   New Rochelle*
*Melbourne   Sydney*

Published by the Press Syndicate of the University of Cambridge
The Pitt Building, Trumpington Street, Cambridge CB2 1RP
32 East 57th Street, New York, NY 10022, USA
296 Beaconsfield Parade, Middle Park, Melbourne 3206, Australia

First published 1984

Printed in the United States of America

*Library of Congress Cataloging in Publication Data*
Rivière, Peter.
Individual and society in Guiana.
(Cambridge studies in social anthropology; 51)
Bibliography: p.
Includes index.
1. Indians of South America – Guiana – Social
conditions.    2. Carib Indians – Social conditions.
3. Social structure – Guiana.    I. Title.    II. Series:
Cambridge studies in social anthropology; no. 51.
F2380.R57    1984     305.8′98′0881      84-7691
ISBN 0 521 26453 7 hard covers
ISBN 0 521 26997 0 paperback

# Contents

v

# Acknowledgments

This book relies very heavily on the information and ideas of others. I am deeply grateful to all the authors whose works form the basis of my own, and above all to those who provided me with additional help and encouragement in the course of conversation and correspondence. The degree of scholarly cooperation that I have received has impressed me greatly. Thus when I say that I accept full and sole responsibility for any misrepresentations and distortions of their works, I mean it with greater sincerity than most such conventional declarations seem to suggest.

I also wish to acknowledge a Personal Research Grant from the Social Science Research Council of Great Britain, which allowed me the time in 1979–80 to lay the foundation of this book.

# 1

# Peoples and approaches

This work has three aims, all of which reflect the present state of ethnographic research in Lowland South America. Although late as an area to receive intensive ethnographic attention, this lateness has not lacked its advantages. Untrammeled by the deadweight of earlier works cast in outmoded anthropological fashions, the ethnography of the area has been characterized in the past decade by an enormous vitality, not only in the quantity of its production but also in the quality of its ideas. It is time to take stock of what we have got and where we stand before pushing on. In a small way, and with reference to only part of the area, this book is intended to be a contribution to that stocktaking.

These remarks are as true for the Northeast region of Lowland South America as they are for the area as a whole, and it is on this region, referred to as "Guiana" and more closely defined below, that attention is focused. Although early accounts by missionaries, travelers, and scientists are often valuable and informative documents, and indeed are the sources for Roth's masterly and comprehensive surveys (1915, 1924, 1929), intensive anthropological fieldwork in the region dates only from the 1930s with Gillin's study (1936) of the Barama River Caribs. After that there was a slight hiatus until Butt, Fock, and Yde started work in the 1950s. Their publications heralded a spate of works that has continued until the present. There is evidence to suggest that we are about to enter a lull in this activity, and, even if this is not so, the time seems ripe to attempt an overview of the rich information now available.

The value of such an exercise must be judged by the aims of this work. In the first place, it is designed to provide an introduction to the region, and I have attempted at this level to fulfill the needs of an undergraduate or postgraduate course on South American Indian ethnography. The second aim, slightly more ambitious, is to identify the essential elements and relationships in Guiana social organization. At this level I am basically addressing my colleagues who work in Guiana and on whose information this study is entirely dependent. Third, and most ambitious of all, I seek to make some suggestions that are relevant to the wider study of Lowland South American society. Work in other regions of the Lowlands has progressed to the point where it is time for similar studies to that

1

undertaken here. At this level, the study is, so to speak, an attempt to provide the Guiana piece in the jigsaw (or mosaic) that forms Lowland South American society. To some extent these three aims are dependent on one another. It is obvious that a competent introduction to the region requires the successful delineation of the essential ingredients. At the same time, failure to portray an accurate picture will undermine the value of the work as a contribution to the wider comparative study.

# I

The region, referred to as Guiana, that is the focus of this book, is the "island" of northeastern South America (see map). It is that area of land surrounded by water: the Amazon River, the Rio Negro, the Casiquiare Canal, the Orinoco River, and the Atlantic Ocean. Its greatest east–west extension is approximately 1,200 miles, and north–south 800 miles. Politically it is divided between Brazil, Venezuela, Guyana, Surinam, and French Guiana. The Amerindians with whom I am concerned live mainly along the watershed that divides the rivers that flow into the Amazon from those that flow into the Orinoco or directly into the Atlantic. The ethnographies from which this study is compiled relate mainly to the Aparaí, the Waiyana, the Trio, the Waiwai, the Wapishiana, the Macusi, the Pemon, the Akawaio, the Ye'cuana, the Piaroa, the Panare, and the Barama River Caribs. There are, however, exceptions to this. For example, the study includes reference to the Maroni River Caribs who live near the coast, but excludes from consideration two of the most populous groups who dwell within the region. These are the Warao and the Yanoama.

The reasons for excluding these two groups are not the same in both cases, although the principle is. It is that they differ in certain quite specific ways from the other groups in the region, although at the same time they share many features. The Warao social organization is characterized by an idol-temple cult reminiscent of the Circum-Caribbean region, an Hawaiian relationship terminology, and a subsistence economy based on the moriche palm pith. The Yanoama group is composed of a number of subgroups, among whom considerable variation exists. Some of these subgroups exhibit a social organization very similar to the other peoples of Guiana, whereas others contain features not found elsewhere. Furthermore, the size as well as the variation makes the Yanoama a highly appropriate subject for a separate study.

To some extent these exclusions are arbitrary but they are not less so than the inclusions, and the selection of Guiana as forming some sort of entity, a subculture of the wider Lowland South America culture area, requires some justification. Before providing this, it must be stressed that there is no assumption that the forms of social organization that characterize the region are not found elsewhere, because they are. Nor is it assumed that the region forms some sort of watertight

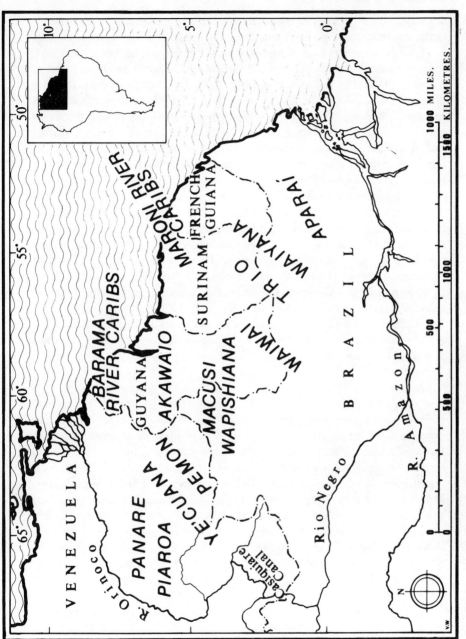

Map of Guiana showing the location of the main Amerindian groups.

cultural compartment with rigid boundaries. It is clear that here as elsewhere in Amazonia boundaries are fuzzy and change unevenly from one region to another.

This is by no means the first time that the Guiana region has been identified as forming a subculture [see, for example, "Handbook of South American Indians," (Steward 1946–50)], and there is no difficulty in indicating the features shared by the people who inhabit the region. In the first place, these similarities are best recognized by what these societies do not have in comparison with those elsewhere in Lowland South America. They lack any formal social groupings such as lineages, clans, moieties, age-sets, etc., membership in which is defined by unilineal descent, name transmission, age, sex, and so on. The social and political organization of these societies is so unformalized that it has often been difficult to understand how they work at all. Over and over again writers have drawn attention to the atomistic nature of these societies and the rampant individualism of their members. Gillin (1936) stresses the individualistic nature of Barama River Carib society and the looseness of its social organization. Butt (1954:33, 44–6) states that the Akawaio have no idea of authority and are characterized by a "great independence of nature." Arvelo-Jimenez (1971:112) refers to the "individualistic tendencies of each Ye'cuana," and Koehn (1975:100) calls the Aparaí "very individualistic." Lapointe (1970) takes the phenomena of the looseness of Waiyana social organization and of their emphasis on individual roles as central to his main concern to explicate the nature of their settlement pattern. Most recently, Thomas (1982:1) has referred to Pemon society as "amorphous."

These societies are rightly described in such terms, but it would be wrong to take a negative view of such a characterization. Pierre Clastres (1977) correctly pointed out that drawing attention to what is absent is a result of our own expectation. If we cannot identify a political organization we must not assume that it is lacking; rather we must accept that we are looking in the wrong place or for the wrong thing and look elsewhere. Thus the looseness of the social organization is not to be seen as the disadvantageous lack of formal institutions but as a positive attribute. If the peoples of Guiana have not developed complex social structures, it is because they have no need for them. It is not because they have not evolved, nor because they are latter-day Noble Savages free of all social constraints. The social organization as it exists provides a fine balance between the requirements of society and the autonomy of the individual. It is the uniformity of ways in which this is achieved that justifies, more than anything else, the selection of the Guiana region as a separable unit of study.

Although each of them will receive detailed attention in later chapters, a brief list of the features of social organization common to the area may be helpful at this point. They include cognatic descent, two-line prescriptive relationship terminology, preferred settlement endogamy and/or uxorilocal residence, the emphasis on co-residence in ordering relationships, and small and impermanent settlements.

4

## Peoples and approaches

The choice of the particular groups to be studied has been largely dictated by the availability of adequate ethnography. The amount and quality of ethnography vary greatly from one group to the next, and although whatever material available has been used it is inevitable that the emphasis has fallen on those people for whom the ethnography is best. Thus the Macusi and Wapishiana receive relatively little attention despite the fact that they are two of the largest groups in the region because we do not know a great deal about them.[1] Sources from the eighteenth, nineteenth, and early twentieth centuries have been used, but I have depended most heavily on material from the last two decades. The reasons for this are simply that most of the earlier writers do not provide the sort of information necessary for a study such as this.

Although many of the recent ethnographers have concentrated on very similar topics, in particular social and political organization, and their works are almost invariably admirably detailed, certain problems still remain in conducting a comparative study. The ethnographers come from different countries, have been brought up in different schools of anthropological thought, and have conducted their research with different aims and expectations. This has led them to express themselves in various ways on what I have had to take to be the same point. To achieve some degree of coherence in my presentation, I have had to translate their ways of putting things in order to achieve a comparison. However, any translation carries the threat of distortion, and where I consider this may be serious I have included an author's own words.

The extent to which the original should be quoted represents another presentational problem in a work of this sort. There is a difficult balance to reach between quoting too much, making the work not only excessively long but little more than a tedious string of quotations, and not citing enough, leaving the less well informed reader at a loss. I hope that a suitable compromise has been reached, and where direct quotation has not been made I have taken care to provide references so that my version can be checked against the original.

Finally, on the matter of the region and its ethnography, I should note that I have not provided a reasoned critique of the sources. Nor have I tried to assess the relative merits of one source against another. This is because the sources mainly refer to different peoples and I have assumed that the differences are a reflection of this fact. Even where we have sources providing rather differing accounts about the same people from a similar period, I have looked for factors that might account for the discrepancies rather than make judgments about their relative correctness. The reason for this is that I am not trying to distill out a single type of Guiana social organization, but rather to reveal the distinctive features of it, both what is variable as well as invariable. At this point, it is important to say a few words about the method involved.

## II

The problem of comparison has been and is of perennial concern to anthropologists. In a general way, comparison is implicit in all their work since any attempt to understand a different way of life or to translate it for one's own kind requires reference to what is familiar. Initially one's own representations act as a model against which to assess another's, although with growing familiarity with the other one can increasingly dispense with one's own world as a point of reference. In this implicit sense, comparison only becomes problematic when the observer's prejudices intrude too far; when they become more than just a preliminary set of instructions by which to orient oneself in an alien world.

Although this represents a threat in any ethnographic endeavor, it is the more explicit forms of comparison, the so-called comparative method, that has proved more problematic. The comparative method has been used in many ways, and it is not my intention to review them here. In general, however, the comparative method has proved a failure either because the goal, such as the establishment of some general sociological law, has been too grandiose and the conclusion too easily undermined, or it has proved difficult to ensure comparability, that like is being compared with like. The remedy for these failings lies in restricting the comparison to a bounded territorial and cultural area, to peoples who exhibit, at least in their gross features, some homogeneity. This approach, usually known as controlled comparison, is more modest in its purpose and seeks, not universal laws, but a better understanding of the localized societies under investigation. However, even the method of controlled comparison is not without its problems, since there is more than one level at which comparison can be conducted.

Thus comparison is possible in terms completely alien to the societies under study. Some external measurement, such as protein supply, is used to compare one group with another in order to explain other variables such as levels of violence and rates of infanticide. Beyond the actual practical difficulties of obtaining reliable measurements of such variables,[2] there are serious epistemological shortcomings in such an approach. There is the difficulty of demonstrating a causal relationship between factors rather than a simple association. The statistical probability of association still leaves unanswered the problem of the negative cases. Then there is no way of incorporating into such explanations human actions and intentions, and such an approach is forced to accept human behavior as guided by external forces.

An alternative way is to conduct the controlled comparison in terms of native categories. In other words, a social category or set of social categories is examined to see how its meaning and content vary among the peoples within a given region and how this variation is related to other differences. This is the approach adopted in the present study, although the comparison has not been confined solely to social groups that bear a linguistic label. For example, although of fundamental importance and readily identifiable in behavioral terms, nowhere in Guiana is there a term for the nuclear family. Likewise it is rare that there is a term for a territorial grouping larger than the single settlement, but it can easily be demonstrated that such groupings exist and have important social, economic, political, and ritual functions. To ignore such unnamed groups would seriously detract from the value of the study for it is possible to show that the failure to recognize the wider social context in which a settlement is contained is consistent with native notions about the nature of the individual settlement.

Although the aim of a controlled comparison, focusing on native categories and behaviors, is to obtain a better understanding of the principles and values ordering the societies concerned, it contains the assumption that this is better done by the comparison of a number of cases rather than the detailed investigation of one. As well as the obvious point that the use of a number of cases acts as a control, there is also the argument that each society reveals to varying degrees and with varying explicitness its organizing principles and values. Like a mosaic, the pattern becomes clearer as each piece is fitted in.

However, the mosaic analogy needs to be used with caution since a priori it is not possible to know whether the societies chosen do form a pattern until some preliminary work has been conducted. This point has been dealt with already. Second, how do we know that the mosaic is bounded? The answer to this is that we do not, nor do we expect it to be. The Guiana region has much in common with other regions of Lowland South America, and the patterns found in Guiana reemerge transformed elsewhere. Thus the Guiana mosaic is simply a piece in a larger mosaic. The third problem is how to know that we have incorporated all the pieces. The answer to this is that we can never be certain that we have taken into account all the variations, but if we have enough variations so that we can identify the principles involved then it is possible to work out all the logical possibilities in order to trace forms that are missing.

There is another important feature that must also be recognized. The pieces are at the same time similar and different. They are similar through being part of the same mosaic; they are different insofar as each is an unique entity, set off from others by particular cultural and social forms. These two properties – which define the relationship of the mosaic to its component pieces – assure simultaneously commonality and separateness. They represent respectively the invariant and variant features.

The aims of this study are relatively modest insofar as it restricts itself mainly to invariant features. This was not the original aim but was the result of concentrating on social structure and social organization. It was assumed that significant variation occurred at these levels; in fact this was found not to be the case. Some variation in social phenomena does occur in the region, and this is documented in the following chapters, but it does not effectively mark off one group from another. The uniqueness of each group is not signaled at the social level, for this, to return to the mosaic analogy, provides the overall pattern. The distinctiveness of each piece, of each group, is expressed through cultural

7

elements. It is through variation in language, body adornments, technical equipment, methods of processing food, funerary rites, and the consumption of hallucinogens that the peoples of Guiana mark themselves off from one another.

There is a problem here of a far greater order than that examined in this book. In principle, I would agree with Lévi-Strauss that

the simplest techniques of any primitive society have hidden in them the character of a system, analysable in terms of a more general system. The manner in which some elements of this system have been retained and others excluded permits us to conceive of the local system as a totality of significant choices, compatible or incompatible with other choices, which each society, or each period within its development, has been led to make. (1967:19)

Although in a study of blowguns and hairtubes (Rivière 1969b), I made an attempt in this direction, in practice a study of cultural variation in these terms is faced with tremendous difficulties. First it is uncertain that the ethnography is good enough for an exercise of this nature to be carried through, since it is often the minutiae of cultural detail that are significant. It is not enough to note that the Trio distinguish themselves both from the Waiyana to the east and the Waiwai to the west by their hairstyle (among other things). It is necessary to know how the choice of a hairstyle, in relationship to other choices, forms a cultural identity.

The second problem is that it appears to be just these cultural elements that are most prone to change, abandonment, and substitution. The readiness to dispense with cultural phenomena does suggest that the boundaries between groups are fluid because their distinctiveness is as transient as the cultural elements that mark it. Certainly the history of the region records a myriad of names that appear and disappear as the groups to which they refer amalgamate and separate, creating a continual flow of new groups. This is in marked contrast with the ability of these groups to retain their social structures through the most adverse conditions.[3] This supports the view that what is fundamental and invariant is the social structure. Further, this invariance can even be seen as a means by which the transience of groups is facilitated; it provides a common basis for the interaction between social groups and a base on which the cultural elements have freedom to vary. Just as the Guiana region does not represent a watertight cultural department, so are these groups not independent tribal units. They are populations whose boundaries are fuzzy as a result of constant interaction through marriage, trade, and migration. We will see that the relationship between settlements, the smallest constituent units of these populations, can be characterized in the same way.

The resolution of the problems concerning the study of cultural variation can be left to the future, although it is a matter that deserves proper attention. For the moment the subject of social invariance is enough, and there is one more aspect that needs to be discussed before moving on. A decision had to be reached on whether the comparative study should be pursued group by group or theme by theme. In the event, it was decided to approach the study theme by theme. There were several reasons for this decision. First, it was decided that by the thematic approach it would be possible both to provide the reader with a more coherent picture and at the same time to develop a more powerful argument. Second, if the groups were treated one by one it would still be necessary to bring the findings together in a series of chapters. Thus the work would be longer without necessarily being any better. Third, because the ethnographies are inevitably uneven in the sense that they do not treat identical topics in the same degree of detail, then the studies of each group would reflect similar tendencies. The approach adopted has been to examine themes or aspects of society in turn. For each aspect those ethnographies that deal with it in the fullest way receive the most attention, and from them a proper picture of the aspect is built up. Then sources that do not devote so much attention to the particular aspect are examined in the light of what is known from the fuller accounts. Because the emphasis on topics differs from one ethnography to another, so the main ethnography used varies from one aspect to another. It is not important for the present purpose whether this variation is the result of the differing interests of the ethnographers themselves or of the emphasis that a given population puts on different aspects. In practice, it is likely to be some of both, although the latter may deserve more weight, because the particular features of the society being studied tend to influence the interests of the ethnographer. What is important is that a more reliable picture can be built up as the study of the same aspect is pursued from one group to the next.

At this point we will leave this rather abstract discussion of method, which is anyway easier to follow in practice, and turn to an introduction to Guiana and its native inhabitants.

## III

It cannot be assumed that all the readers of this volume will be familiar with Guiana and its native inhabitants, and because the main body of the study presupposes this knowledge some attempt to remedy any such deficiency is made here. The description that follows is both broad and general. Some of the topics touched upon are dealt with in far greater detail in later chapters, whereas others receive no further attention although acquaintance with them will help in understanding the argument. Those already familiar with the region can afford to miss this section.

The native peoples with whom we are concerned live on the pre-Cambrian Guiana Highlands, a peneplain that is the predominant geological feature of the region. The rivers that originate in these Highlands are, with the exception of the Orinoco River, small by the standards of Lowland South America. Broken by series of rapids at the point where they leave the peneplain, these rivers do not offer good lines of communication and easy access into the interior. Furthermore, because of the nature of the seasonal cycle, there are times of the year when the waterways are little more than fordable streams and other times when they are rushing torrents that flood out over the surrounding terrain to head height. The flatness of the watershed in some areas results in extensive flooding during the wet season.

Although there is some variation across the region, the year is basically marked by two seasons, wet and dry. The dry season lasts approximately from September to March and the wet season from April to August. In some parts the wet season extends almost to December, whereas in others a brief wet season occurs around December-January so that four seasons, two wet and two dry, divide the year. The dry season is rarely completely dry, nor the wet season devoid of dry days. The amount of rainfall fluctuates greatly from one year to the next, but on average everywhere gets 2,000 mm or more a year. The mean annual temperature is around 26 degrees centigrade, with the dry season the hottest time of the year. The diurnal range of temperature is much greater than the annual range.

Although tropical forest is the predominant type of vegetation, stretches of savanna occur, and to the north and west of the region these are extensive. However, even when Amerindians are found dwelling on these grasslands, they always do so in proximity to forest, which occurs as galleries along watercourses or as cover on the low hills.

A list of the groups with which this study is primarily concerned has been provided already. With the exception of the Arawakan Wapishiana and the Sáliban Piaroa, all these peoples are Carib speaking. Basso (1977) has isolated eight traits that she regards as typically Carib; although not all these traits are dealt with in this work, they occur in most of the societies considered. Indeed, here as elsewhere in Lowland South America, linguistic differences do not necessarily coincide with social and cultural differences, although it is not unusual for the Indians themselves to use variations in dialect to make social distinctions.

All the peoples of the area are slash-and-burn cultivators. The main cultigen and dietary staple is bitter cassava. This crop is supplemented by a wide range of other produce, including sweet cassava, sweet potatoes, yams, eddoes, peanuts, maize, bananas, sugarcane, pineapples, and peppers. Nonedible cultivated plants include tobacco, cotton, silk grass, gourds, arrowcane, and urucu. Compared with forms of slash-and-burn cultivation found elsewhere the technique is fairly crude. Tree stumps and large unburnt trunks are left where they are, and secondary clearing is often reduced to a minimum, as are weeding and other cultivation practices. The main crop, cassava, is usually planted twice, the second planting taking place as the first crop is harvested. Fields go on producing for about four years, but after they have been abandoned they are often still visited in order to pick cotton and bananas. The usual practice is to start a new field each year so that a family normally has two fields, at different stages in their life cycles, producing simultaneously. The reasons for abandoning a field are

10

numerous and include competition from weeds and secondary growth, infestation by pests (such as leaf-cutting ants), and relocation of the settlement itself.

The cutting and burning of the forest are everywhere men's work, and men do most of the secondary clearing. Women participate in the planting, and from this point in the agricultural cycle women take over the responsibility of caring for the field, harvesting, and replanting. Women are also responsible for the processing of cultivated foods, in particular of bitter cassava, which is a long-drawn-out and time-consuming business. The main products of cassava are bread and drink.

The main contribution by men to the diet is meat from hunting and fishing. Where rivers are large enough, fishing tends to take precedence over hunting. The gathering of forest produce also plays an important part in the total economy, although perhaps less so among those peoples who have been exposed to outside contacts. Gathering, performed by both men and women, contributes both to the diet (wild fruits, honey, etc.) and provides the raw materials for the manufacture of material culture items from houses to bows and pots to baskets.

Diet and nutrition among the peoples of the region have been studied little, but the impression is that they are of a high standard and require relatively little expenditure of time. Hurault's work (1965) on the Waiyana supports this view, as does Hames's (1978, 1980) and Hames and Vickers's (1982) on the Ye'cuana. The heated discussions of the last decade on the impact of protein supply on the size and distribution of settlements look as though they are being resolved in favor of the view that protein is not in short supply and is not the crucial factor in determining the settlement pattern.

Settlements consist of either a single longhouse (usually round and conical shaped) or one or more smaller shed-type dwellings. The basic structure is a wood-frame with palm-leaf thatch, which in certain types of house reaches down to the ground. Walls of clay and wattle are found, and houses may be left open. Settlements are small, relatively widely dispersed, and impermanent. Various reasons are given for moving a village, including deterioration of the houses due to old age, infestation by weeds and pests, death in the settlement, distance from fields as land close at hand gets used up, and because other natural resources prove inadequate. Membership of villages is not fixed, and there is considerable movement between settlements.

The division of labor is mainly organized along sexual lines, although age has some importance. Given the sexual division of labor and a technology that rarely requires the cooperative efforts of several members of the same sex, it is broadly true to say that an adult man and woman are a self-sufficient unit, capable between them of all productive and reproductive tasks. The nuclear family is therefore a significant unit in the social organization, and one to which even young children contribute in a variety of ways, from baby minding to the provision of small fish. However, it is rare for the nuclear family to be isolated from other kin, and it often forms a unit within a vertically or horizontally

11

extended family. The relationship between siblings is important, and the core of any settlement is often composed of a set of siblings. The frequency with which mothers and daughters, and/or sisters, are found living together gives the region a matrilateral flavor that led many early writers to call these groups matrilineal. In fact, the rule of descent is everywhere cognatic. There is a preference for village endogamy, but the small size of settlements rarely permits this. The usual alternative is uxorilocal residence, at least for a period. The relationship terminologies, and kinship is the idiom of social interaction, are in every case two-line and articulated by prescriptive exchange. The prescribed category every-where includes the bilateral cross-cousin, although it may also include other genealogically defined individuals as well as those with whom no genealogical relationship can be traced.

The individual life cycle is marked by rites of passage, and such rites as well as other periodic rituals often require the participation of the inhabitants of more than one community. Ritual also forms an essential part of many technical activities, such as preparing a garden site or processing food. Overall, however, and compared with other peoples of Lowland South America, ritual activity in the region is relatively low key. The necessity for ritual in everyday life combined with an unequal distribution of proficiency in its practice creates a dependency that cements individuals, families, and communities into the wider social world.

Although individuals differ in their competence in and preference for certain activities, there is no specialization as such. The exception to this is the shaman, whose ability to communicate with the invisible world is the outcome of a difficult and dangerous apprenticeship. In Guiana, unlike some other regions, the shaman has the monopoly on contact with the spirit world, and shamanistic experience is not a necessary part of adulthood. Although a shaman's activities may be restricted in various ways and at certain times, he is not normally freed from the routine subsistence tasks. However, because of his privileged relation-ship with the invisible world the shaman wields political power, even to the point that in certain cases shamanistic knowledge is the qualification for village leadership. The relationship between headmanship and shamanism is a variable that appears to be dependent on the degree to which ritual knowledge is regarded as an essential but scarce resource. This, in turn, varies with cosmological ideas, and although this topic is touched upon the proper attention it undoubtedly deserves has been left for a later study.

Whether a headman requires shamanistic expertise or not, the other qualities he needs include competence in routine affairs, generosity, and persuasive talk. A headman also needs a network of close kinsmen. The weakness of the headman's position springs from his lack of coercive sanctions and of absolute control over any scarce resource. The general availability of the necessities of life from the environment, and the absence of the notion of territoriality or landownership, allow for a high level of mobility between settlements. Furthermore, each settlement is an autonomous unit, and there are no overarching political institutions. A headman's authority, weak enough in his own village, spreads no further than that.

This background to the region would not be complete without a few words on its history, particularly with reference to these groups' contact with nonindigenous peoples. The experiences of these groups have been so different that it is not possible to generalize about them. The earliest contacts, and by this is meant "recorded" contact, occurred for the Wapishiana, Macusi, and Pemon by the mid-eighteenth century, whereas for the Waiwai and Trio it was almost one hundred years later. In the case of the Macusi and Wapishiana, first contact was quickly followed by permanent contact, whereas the Trio have only experienced this within the last generation. As a result of contact, whether permanent or sporadic, two very important changes occurred; one in the sphere of demography, the other in the area of technology.

Although we have no way of knowing the scale of demographic decline, there is every reason to believe that it was substantial. The causes of it were imported diseases against which the Indians had no resistance and the effects of which could still be observed among the Trio two decades ago, and the enslaving and transportation of the people. The difficulty is that we do not know what effect this drop in population had on these societies. Some accounts of first encounters with groups [such as those of Schomburgk (1841, 1845) on the Waiwai and Trio] describe the distribution and size of settlement as similar to that recorded one hundred years later, but one must not forget that disease, transmitted through Indians, could have started to take its toll ahead of the arrival of the first European. At the moment, the situation has reversed itself, and throughout the whole region populations are growing dramatically.

The other important item introduced by Europeans was manufactured goods, in particular metal-cutting tools, axes, knives, and machetes. Because of the extensive native trading networks these goods, in limited quantities, found their way into the remotest places long before Europeans got there. Once again we do not know what impact this new technology had on the socioeconomic organization. It is obvious that it must have reduced enormously the time and effort required to clear a field. But what we do not know is whether before the introduction of metal goods fields were smaller and whether there was less reliance on cultivated foods, of which shortage was experienced;[4] or whether fields in the past were smaller but adequate so that the present larger fields provide a wider margin of safety or a bigger surplus that may be consumed in ritual and political activity; or whether fields in the past were the same size as those today and men have gained a lot of extra free time. What we do know is that the availability of manufactured goods has brought about a certain amount of population movement in order to improve access to them. However, what does not appear to have happened is control by certain individuals over the supply of such highly valued goods. If this had happened, the political structure of the region would have undergone some drastic changes.

13

There is not much in the following chapters about the nonindigenous peoples of the region, but there is no pretense that all the Amerindians of the region are not in permanent relationship, of one or several sorts, with such peoples. For the purpose of the present study this is regarded as a constant, although clearly there is a fascinating study to be made of the responses and reactions of different groups to the forms of contact that they have experienced.

**IV**

The order in which this study is presented is determined by the wish to move from the more concrete to the less concrete, on the grounds that this is the direction most easily followed by the reader. Accordingly, a start is made in Chapter 2 by examining the only geographical and physical manifestation of the Guiana social order: the settlement – its size, duration, and distribution. From this, we move on to consider in Chapter 3 the settlement as a social unit, both in terms of its ideal and actual composition. This leads to an account in Chapter 4 of the social categories from which Guiana society is constituted. Chapter 4 ends with a consideration of marriage rules and practices. In Chapter 5, the nature and content of the relationships between the more important social categories are discussed. The autonomous nature of the settlement over and against its dependency on other settlements forms the subject matter of Chapter 6. The nature of politics, the role of the individual, and problems of social continuity are looked at in Chapter 7. In the final chapter, an attempt is made to generalize about Guiana society in the context of Lowland South America.[5]

# 2

# The settlement pattern: size, duration, and distribution

## I

In Chapter 1 the point was made that it is a mistake to characterize the indigenous societies of the Guianas in terms of what they lack. Even so, it is true to say that the absence of any formal social groupings that could act as pegs on which to hang a description makes the problem of presentation that much more difficult. The closest one can get to identifying a social group that has any sort of corporate existence is the inhabitants of a single settlement. Even this is not entirely satisfactory, for these groups have only a transitory presence. Settlements are short-lived, and even within their lifetime their populations, and thus the composition of the group, undergo continual change as people come and go. But, ephemeral as settlements are, to focus on them is an approach that allows an initial glimpse of fleeting stability in a fluid and relative world. It is in the formation, composition, and dispersion of settlements, apparently so chaotic, that it is possible to observe the range of choices that the social structure makes available to the individual, and beyond them to the very principles by which the social structure itself is articulated. Thus a suitable place to start this study is with settlement size, duration, and distribution.

First, however, it is necessary to indicate that the term "settlement" cannot be used to refer to the same thing throughout the region. There are those people (Waiwai, Ye'cuana, Piaroa, and Panare) whose settlements usually consist of a single communal dwellinghouse. There are those (Trio, Waiyana) who live in nucleated villages composed of a number of houses.[1] There is the pattern uniquely exemplified by the Akawaio, who have nucleated central villages with dispersed houses located at distant garden sites. Compared with these patterns, the Macusi, Wapishiana, and Pemon, all of whom live on the savanna, exhibit a more variegated arrangement. Whereas nucleated villages do exist, dispersed houses are the more common occurrence. In the majority of cases, native terms exist that have the meaning of settlement, but as these terms often also have social and political connotations they will be considered in Chapter 3 and later rather than here. As well as the single settlement, some peoples recognize the existence of and have a term for larger units. Even in those cases where no term exists, it is often possible to discern such units both by their geographical discreteness and by the behavior and attitudes of their inhabitants.

Second, the information relating to settlement size, duration, and distribution is uneven in its quality, quantity, and historical depth. However, it is not the present purpose to review all the information on these topics nor to provide an historical account of population changes. Rather, it is to give as accurate a picture as possible using the most reliable and specific information available. The historical dimension is not ignored but its incorporation presents certain difficulties because the peoples concerned have been submitted to different types and lengths of European contact. For example, the Macusi and Wapishiana have been in permanent contact for close on two centuries, whereas the Trio have only experienced this within the lifetime of the present generation. Nor can we allow for the unrecorded events and changes, such as migration, disease, and slave raiding, resulting from indirect contact. For example, we may assume that until around the middle of this century and in some cases until more recently all the populations of the region were declining. In most cases this process has been halted, and in some dramatically reversed. It is difficult to assess the exact influence of these fluctuating demographic fortunes on the settlement patterns and other features of social organization.

## II

Discussion of this topic can usefully begin with the Waiyana because the information relating to them is not only detailed but also has an historical depth that is rarely encountered in the region. The first recorded European visitor to the Waiyana was Patris in 1766 and 1769 who, beyond stating that they are numerous, describes a remarkably centralized government with the fortified village of the supreme chief containing perhaps as many as 400 people (Tony 1843:225). Twenty years later, when Leblond visited the Waiyana, this political organization seems to have disappeared, but he refers to 24 Waiyana villages spread out along forest trails about eight miles apart, and the total Waiyana population as 3,000; an average of 165 to a village (Hurault 1968:2).

There is then a gap of almost one hundred years before further information is forthcoming. Crevaux visited the Waiyana in 1877, but is not particularly helpful about the subject matter of this chapter. Better in this respect is Coudreau, who was in the region ten years later. Coudreau estimated there to be between 1,000 and 1,500 Waiyana distributed among 35 (1893:547) or 36 villages (p. 566). This gives an average figure somewhere between 29 and 43 people to a village. Although he rarely gives the actual number of Indians found in any particular village, the most he mentions is 60, including many travelers (p. 82), and the fewest 25 (p. 540).

Although Coudreau's information has often been regarded with suspicion,

16

there are no grounds for doing so with regard to these figures because they coincide with those provided by the more reliable Dutchman, de Goeje. De Goeje reckoned there to be 23 villages and 1,000 Waiyana at the time of the Tumuchumac expedition in 1907, and as a result of a return trip thirty years later he revised these figures to 600 Indians in 20 villages, each containing 10 to 50 people (1941:72, 121).

The first detailed census of the Waiyana was made by Schmidt during the course of several journeys in 1940–42. He visited 16 Waiyana villages and heard of 4 others. The total population he reckoned at 358, or an average of 17 inhabitants to a village. Of the villages he visited, the smallest contained 7 inhabitants and the largest 31 (1942:50–5). In 1948–9, Sausse estimated a similar total, of whom 150 were living on the River Itany and the remainder in Brazil. He further noted that the Itany Waiyana were distributed among 4 villages, 3 of which on the French bank contained 61 Indians between them. This left the other 89 living in one village on the Surinam side of the river; a concentration that may be accounted for by the existence of goldworkings (1951:100–1).

The most complete recent information on the Waiyana is provided in a series of publications by Hurault, who made various expeditions to the Maroni Basin between 1948 and 1965. He gave a total of 400 Waiyana in 1958, of which 240 lived in the Upper Maroni divided between 8 villages. No village contained more than 45 inhabitants, and the average is 30 to a village (1961:142–3; 1963:114). At a slightly later date, he claimed that most Waiyana villages contained between 15 and 60 people (1965:22). More detailed information was available about the situation in 1964, when he revised his figure upward to a total of 650–700 Waiyana, of whom 260 lived on the Itany, 100 in the Paloemeu, 200 on the Yari, and 200 on the Paru (1968:3). At that time, the Itany River Waiyana were dispersed in 11 villages, an average of 23–4 Indians to a village. Although we are not told the size of any village population, we are given the number of families in each village. It is thus possible to work out a crude figure. There were 66 families in the 11 villages, which suggests that an average family was composed of four people. The smallest village contained 2 families or 8 people, and the largest 16 families or 64 people. However, the largest village was located at a mission station and it is safe to assume that it was artificially large. If we ignore this village, the next largest contained 8 families or 32 people, and the average is about 5 families or 20 people to a village (1968:5).

Later, in the 1960s, Lapointe worked with the Waiyana of the Paru de Leste in Brazil. At the time there were 14 villages on that river, 4 of which contained mainly Aparaí and 10 mainly Waiyana. The total population was 161 Indians, an average of approximately 12 people to a village, with size ranging from 2 to 35 (1970:14).[2]

Lapointe also provides some evidence on the distribution of these villages. They occupy a 150–mile stretch of river, and, with the exception of two villages 20 minutes apart, the others are separated by about 10 miles or a day's upstream paddling (1970:14–15). Although, except for Leblond's eighteenth-century statement that Waiyana villages were 8 miles apart, no author gives precise information on the distances between villages, it is perfectly clear from all the publications mentioned and others that Waiyana villages are fairly widely dispersed, rarely less than a half-day's walk or paddle from one another. It is also apparent that the Waiyana now, if not in the past, form four distinct local groups, which are located respectively in the Maroni, Tapanahoni, East Paru, and Yari river basins.

Comments on the duration of villages also tend to be of a general and imprecise nature. For example, Coudreau simply states that villages are relocated frequently (1893:84). Sausse says that on average villages are moved every five to six years (1951:103), whereas Lapointe, referring to the difficulties involved in getting accurate information on the length of occupation of a given site, suggests that it is from five or six years to fifteen with an average of seven or eight (1970:81).

Hurault twice states that villages rarely remain more than ten years in the same place, and on average they are relocated every five to six years (1965:24; 1968:4). Unfortunately, however, the more detailed information on the movement of Waiyana villages on the Itany between 1948 and 1962 (1965:facing p. 24) needs to be treated with caution and not accepted as typical because of the operation of external forces in the shape of the availability of work and manufactured goods. It may be noted that within that fourteen-year period every village moved once and half of them twice. Furthermore, many of these movements were to sites close at hand.

The Waiyana case has been dealt with in some detail because, with over two hundred years of information available, it is particularly instructive. The eighteenth-century sources give a picture of a people more numerous and living in larger villages than they were one hundred years later. Since the end of the last century village size, between 20 and 40 inhabitants, has remained fairly constant while the population and number of villages have declined.

The Trio group will be treated more briefly, for although there are references earlier than this century they provide no information of the sort that concerns us here. The Dutch expeditions of the first decade of this century are also disappointing from this point of view because although the published reports give the first good account of the Trio, they contain little information of a demographic nature. Bakhuis, who visited two villages in the eastern part of Trio territory, states that they contained 30 to 40 people each (1908:110). A decade later, Farabee passed through two Diau[3] villages in the western part. A dance was in progress at one of these villages, to which most of the members from the other village had gone. The combined population of both villages can be computed at 53, and since both villages contained the same number of dwellinghouses one may assume that their respective populations were about equal, around 26 each (1924:200–2).

## Settlement pattern: size, duration, distribution

Schmidt in his travels in the early 1940s visited 21 Trio villages and was told of the existence of 4 others. He estimated there to have been 687 Trio with an average of 27–8 people to a village. The largest village he saw contained 47 Indians and the smallest 8 (1942:50, 55–62). Frikel, who started his missionary travels in the area a decade later, agrees broadly with Schmidt about the average size of village, but puts the total number of Indians at 1,000 to 1,200 and claims that Schmidt overlooked at least 15 villages (Frikel and Cortez 1972:38–9). Frikel also states that villages rarely exceed 50 people (1973:13).

The upheavals in the settlement pattern brought about by missionary activity in the early 1960s were far enough advanced by the time of my own fieldwork to have obscured the traditional picture, and reconstruction of it proved unfeasible. However, it is interesting to note that in recent years there has been some dispersion away from the mission villages, both in Brazil and Surinam. The four new settlements that have grown up all contain between 20 and 30 inhabitants.

Although attempts to reconstruct the composition of individual villages proved unsatisfactory, analysis of the material did reveal the existence of three local groups, each composed of a number of villages and centered on different river basins. Furthermore, within these river-basin groups, a number of villages forming distinct clusters could also be identified (Rivière 1969a:35–7). Although the Trio have no terms for these groupings and do not explicitly recognize them, they were found to have important social and political implications (Rivière 1969a:108; 1971). The analysis rested in part on my own data but also essentially on information contained in Schmidt (1942). It showed that villages of the same cluster were never more than a day's walk apart, but that the nearest villages of different clusters were separated by two days' march and those of different river-basin groups by about three or four days.

The evidence on the duration of villages is less certain. De Goeje says villages lasted for five to ten years (1908:1120), whereas Frikel says no more than that there is a regular shift of the village site (1973:14). That village sites are moved with relative frequency is further borne out by the number of abandoned villages reported by the various Dutch expeditions at the beginning of the century and by Schmidt. A point made by de Goeje (1908:1120), Frikel (1973:14) and Schmidt (1942:32), and supported by my own observations and those of members of the missionary organization in Surinam, is that villages were often moved only short distances.

We can conclude that Trio villages normally contained 20 to 40 people, were fairly well spaced out, and had a life span of only a few years, although new villages were often built at no great distance from the old.

Data from the Waiwai group are available from the second quarter of the last century. Schomburgk was the first person to visit the area, and in 1837 he saw two Taruma villages (one of 60 people, the other of 20), a Barokoto village of 40 inhabitants, and three Waiwai villages of which the estimated total population was 150 (1841:166–71). Seven years later, on his second journey, he noted a Taruma village of "upwards of 50" people including some visitors (1845:43), and a mixed Mawayenna/Taruma village of 60 (1845:55).

Farabee, who was there in 1913, recorded a mixed Barokoto/Waiwai village of 34 people (1924:176); in his *Central Arawaks*, he gives the populations of three villages as 34, 44, and 42 without indicating whether they were Wapishiana, Atorai, Taruma, or Mawayenna villages (1918:172). In 1937, Holden visited Waiwai villages on both sides of the Sierra Acarai and stated that each settlement contained 25 to 30 people (1938:329).

Meggers and Evans, while doing archaeological work in the region in 1952–3, took the opportunity to record some ethnographic notes. At that time there were four Waiwai villages in the Upper Essequibo, of which the populations were respectively 14, 11, 18, and 16 (1964:201–4).[4] A few years later, in 1955–6, the Danish anthropologists Fock and Yde undertook intensive fieldwork among the Waiwai. They found on the Essequibo three villages with 41, 26, and 13 inhabitants repectively (Yde 1965:5–9). On the Brazilian side of the Sierra Acarai there were four more villages, a small one of only 7 people, whereas the others contained 20 to 40 each (Fock 1963:4).[5] It is clear from Fock's account that the Waiwai were divided into two distinct groups, one in the Upper Essequibo and the other in the Upper Mapuera, with nine days' travel between them compared with one and a half or two and a half days' travel between the most distant villages within the river-basin group (1963:4). When Yde returned to the area in 1958, this pattern had completely disappeared as a result of missionary influence (1965:19).

Once again, although there is no observational evidence on the average life span of villages, it is clear that villages were moved frequently. One can point to the numerous sites investigated by Evans and Meggers, many of which had been occupied several times (1960), and the abandoned settlements recorded by Yde (1965:11–13).[6]

There is nothing in the Waiwai evidence that is out of line with the peoples already examined. Villages tended to have between 20 and 40 inhabitants (although they were rather larger in the last century), rarely rising much above the higher figure and infrequently dropping below 10. The settlements were dispersed and appear to have had a relatively short but unspecified life span.

The groups living on the savannas will be dealt with later, and we will turn first to the peoples living in the more forested region of southern Venezuela. The Ye'cuana, although living in an area of mixed forest and savanna, inhabit with few exceptions the former environment. The main source here is Arvelo-Jimenez, who provides population figures for 21 villages. If we ignore 2 villages whose populations have been artificially swollen by the presence of mission stations, the size of villages ranged from 7 to 81 people, with over half the settlements containing between 30 and 60 inhabitants (1971:54–6).

These figures agree well with two reliable historical sources. First, in 1838–9

## Settlement pattern: size, duration, distribution

Schomburgk visited 5 Ye'cuana villages and recorded that they contained 50, 32, 19, 23, and 64 inhabitants, respectively (1841a:224–37). At the beginning of this century, Koch-Grünberg noted that Ye'cuana villages contained between 20 and 70 souls, although it was not always easy to distinguish inhabitants from guests (1923:322). However, de Barandiaran (1966:49–51) gives the impression of more populous settlements, with the number of inhabitants in a single house reaching as many as 120.

Arvelo-Jimenez analyzes village size and claims that it is related to a village's degree of maturity. Incipient villages range in size from 8 to 27 people; a village on the point of reaching "stability as an autonomous community" contains 40 to 50 people; and mature villages have a population of 50 to 70, after which point they begin to lose people (1971:61). Elsewhere (1973) the same author has argued that Ye'cuana settlements vary in size as a result of external pressure; in particular, they tend to become smaller and more numerous in the face of hostile threats.

The ethnographer is equally explicit on the subject of settlement distribution, and she is worth quoting on the matter: "Each village is at least a full day's journey away from the next, but most of them are even further apart. There is more regular visiting and feasting among those villages which lie along the same river. Thus, villages can be referred to as belonging to certain 'river areas'" (1971:14). She later claims that although the Ye'cuana give a generic term to all people located on the same river, the name often being derived from that of the river, this is purely a geographic reference without political or social connotations. On the other hand, de Barandiaran states that settlements are two, three, four, or more days' travel apart (1966:49–51).

On the subject of village duration, Arvelo-Jimenez is equally precise: "Villages are highly mobile units. Even a relatively stable village changes its location every five years. Others remain on the same site only one or two years" (1971:92).

The information on the Ye'cuana is among the most definite we have, and it is interesting that village size has remained remarkably constant over a period of 130 years.

The Piaroa case is also very straightforward, although there is among them the recognition of a two-tier pattern, a village and a local group. The village, *itso'de*, is normally composed of a single communal dwelling inhabited by 15 to 50 people. A number of *itso'de* (anything from 2 to 10) combine to form the local group, *itso'fha*. Within the *itso'fha* the *itso'de* are about a half-day's walk apart, although other patterns occur; for example, the *itso'de* may be very much more closely spaced, even sharing the same clearing (Kaplan 1975:29). Sites are inhabited at the most for ten years, and the distance away a new settlement is located may be a matter of yards or miles, depending on the reason for the move (Kaplan 1975:57–8). The boundaries of the *itso'fha* do not appear to be any more stable than the location of individual *itso'de*, and the latter, without moving its site, may change its *itso'fha* affiliation.

21

The pattern we have so far described was also characteristic of the Barama River Caribs when Gillin visited them in the 1930s. He describes their settlements as varying from 7 to 70 individuals; the one village (Sawari) for which he provides details had 47 inhabitants (1936:98, 106). There are reasons to suspect that at the time of Gillin's visit this village was in the process of fission, for it had recently divided into three distinct, although closely located, settlements as a result of internal disputes. The three villages nearest to Sawari were respectively 3 to 5, 6, and 12 hours' walk away. On the question of village duration Gillin is not specific, but he estimated that Sawari was ten years old at the time of his stay, and indicates that change of residence was not uncommon (1936:139, 31–2). By 1969, when Adams restudied the Barama River Caribs, this settlement pattern had been disrupted by developments in the river basin, in particular mining, missions, and government programs. The overall effect had been a concentration of the population around such developments (Adams 1972:ch. 3).

The Barama River Caribs' Guyana neighbors, the Akawaio, reveal an interesting adaptation to the problem of concentration. Their settlement pattern is characterized by more or less permanent central villages (in some cases over one hundred years old), which are ringed at up to a day's walk away by temporary garden places (of five to six years' duration). The inhabitants of a garden place, usually consisting of an extended family, rarely number more than 15, whereas the main settlement will vary between 20 and 60 people depending on how many are away at their garden places at any particular moment. Butt explains the movements between the different localities both in terms of responses to economic, including seasonal, requirements, and also to social, political, and ritual factors (Butt 1970:36–42).

The Panare live in an area of mixed forest and savanna, and seasonal movements between these different environments are also a feature of their settlement pattern. J.-P. Dumont and Henley agree on the basic features of the Panare settlement pattern, although their terminologies differ. Dumont states that villages vary in size from 30 to 60 people (1976:13), although he later gives examples of smaller villages (16 and 17 people) and refers to villages of "above sixty individuals" (1978:72–3, 76). Henley recognizes two levels in the settlement pattern. First there is the "settlement group" (which seems to correspond to Dumont's settlement), and second what he calls "communities," which are composed of one or more settlements (1979:32). In 1975–6, 38 communities existed, and the total population of these is estimated at 1,708 (with an error of plus or minus 202) (1979:52–5). The size of these communities varies between 19 and 226, the largest consisting of 10 settlements (1979:32). However, if one leaves to one side the 4 largest communities, all of which are influenced by extraneous factors and contain 226, 130, 90, and 90 people, respectively, the sizes of the remaining communities correspond with that given by Dumont for his settlements, with 25 containing between 25 and 40 inhabitants. To put a shallow historical perspective on these figures, it may be noted that they agree with those

22

from 6 *aldeas* collected by Wilbert in 1957. Four of these villages had between 25 and 43 inhabitants, one had 87, and another 11 (1963:24).

The distribution of settlements, even prior to its disruption by neo-Venezuelan and missionary intrusion, is slightly more complex than that so far described. Henley notes that the usual and traditional pattern of Panare residence was to live in dispersed main settlements in the forested mountains with temporary houses down on the plains (1979:61; see also map 4) and that the Indians make "shifts of a few kilometres . . . every three or four years" (1979:84). J.-P. Dumont states that "settlements are separated from one another by no less than 15 km, or a two-hour walking distance" (1976:13). He gives no average figure for the duration of a settlement, although he does say that when it is a matter solely of the aging of the house and the increasing distance of the fields, a new site will be found "after about eight to ten years" (p. 13). Dumont also treats at some length the movement of the Panare between different types of habitation on a daily and seasonal basis (pp. 67–89), although he tends to stress the symbolic underpinning of these relocations more than the economic and social aspects.

In summary, Panare settlements contain as a rule between 25 and 40 people, are relatively dispersed, are of short duration, and have inhabitants who tend to separate and gather together again according to season.

The remaining groups that come within the orbit of this study are all savanna dwellers, and in many ways their settlement pattern presents a rather different picture from those so far considered. The best described case is that of the Pemon, and it does raise the question of what constitutes a settlement. Simpson (1940:380–4) makes it clear that the Pemon Kamarakoto do not have villages as such, but groups of dispersed but associated dwellings. The figures he gives for the central Kamarakoto region indicate a population of approximately 250 living in 26 such groups, an average of around 10 people to the group (1940:364–7). A census taken in 1937 and covering all the Pemon arrived at a figure of 1,084 living in 145 houses, an average of just over 7 to a house (quoted in Layrisse and Wilbert 1966:82).

The most detailed and up-to-date information on the central Pemon is that provided by Thomas (1973), who usefully compares his figures with those from the 1937 census. The population for the area with which Thomas is concerned had increased over threefold, but there had been no significant change in the size of households. Instead, there are now more settlements and a larger proportion of settlements now contain more than one household. Indeed, the number of settlements has doubled whereas the proportion of multihousehold settlements has increased from 33 to 55 percent (1973:61–4).

Settlements are located at varying distances from one another, and although they are not recognized by the Pemon as forming groups, the ethnographer has been able to identify a number of zones on the basis of the density of genealogical ties and the intensity of intersettlement visiting. At the same time, the Pemon do differentiate between various regions and refer to people by the region from which they come (1973:82, 99, 108–9). Although population mobility appears to be as high as elsewhere, it is not uncommon for a settlement to remain in the same locality for long periods, up to twenty years. This, as much as anything, seems to reflect the Pemon's willingness to exploit resources over a wide area, and gardens are often cut at a considerable distance from the savanna-located settlement (1982:34, 46).

In 1978, Urbina made a brief investigation of a single Pemon Arecuna settlement. Urbina notes that this settlement – with 114 inhabitants dwelling in 14 houses – is exceptionally large and considers a traditional settlement rarely to surpass 40 people (1979:25). However, in terms of average household size, Urbina's data (8 to a house) coincide with the figures already referred to and affirm a remarkable constancy of Pemon household size over nearly a half-century of rapidly changing conditions.

There appear to be no data on this topic for the Wapishiana, but from Diniz's material (1972:ch. 4) it is possible to work out that the average size of domestic groups in 9 Macusi settlements was 7.8 people. Once again, this figure fits remarkably well with that for the Pemon. On the other hand, from my own casual observations in Guyana and Brazil, the Macusi settlement pattern is rather different from that of the Pemon, and most Macusi live in nucleated settlements. There appear to be various explanations for this, including access to educational and employment opportunities, but perhaps the major reason is the pressure on land brought about by the development of cattle ranching. At the same time, both the Macusi and the Wapishiana have garden places in the forest-covered hills, and the substantial shelters to be found in them suggest that part of the year is spent in residence at the garden place.

Finally, in this section, it will be useful to examine what information there is, and it is scant, on the rate of population mobility between settlements. Hurault provides some information on the Waiyana of the Itany River. He computed that approximately 28 percent of these Indians changed residence in 1958. From 1958 to 1964, 15 to 20 percent a year moved within the Itany region, and a further 2 to 5 percent a year changed from one river group to another (1968:73). For the Parú Waiyana, Lapointe gives the rather lower figure of 9 percent of the population moving annually (1970:78). There are no other figures by which to judge how typical these are, but the general impression given by most ethnographers is that the rate of population mobility is fairly high. Although the statistical evidence on this topic is poor, many writers provide histories of settlements or accounts of particular events in which are detailed who moved and why. This invaluable information is central to our understanding of the settlement as a political entity.

## III

The subject of settlement patterns has been treated at some length because it is considered essential to provide a secure factual and numerical base for the argument that follows. To end this chapter we wish to devote some space to certain preliminary comments about relationships of settlement patterns to ecological, social, political, and cultural factors.

The material presented in this last section indicates that the Guiana region is characterized by two basic settlement patterns, one associated with the forest, the other with the savanna. In the former, villages average around 30 inhabitants, with the usual range being 15 to 50, although settlements larger than this are not uncommon. The minimum distance between villages is on the order of a half-day's walk, and in those cases where local groups composed of a number of related villages within a defined geographical area exist, the distance between such groups may be several days' travel. Villages, with certain exceptions, never last long on the same site; more than ten years is unusual and the average duration seems closer to six or seven years, with even shorter periods not being uncommon. A new village site is often close to that of the abandoned settlement, and more often than not where extensive movements have occurred and traditional areas been abandoned some outside influence is usually to blame. Finally, population is readily, if not highly, mobile.

The savanna people share many of these features, the crucial difference being that settlements on average contain fewer inhabitants, although even here large villages do occur, and the usual upper range is lower.

The Akawaio pattern with its central village and outlying garden sites represents a further variant, but there is reason to believe that this is a relatively recent development that has occurred in response to new cultural factors. A similar pattern in embryonic form can be seen developing among the Trio as a result of their adaptation to external agencies.

A start to the discussion can be made by looking at the factors that exert some influence on the minimum and maximum sizes of settlements. The minimum size of settlements is not a topic that has concerned many ethnographers. Most authors have noted that the smallest viable economic unit consists of an adult man and woman,[7] and in the short term this is true. There are plenty of examples in the literature of settlements whose population consists of no more than a single nuclear family. However, there are factors that militate against such isolationism, and these are mainly of a demographic, social, and cultural nature. Hurault claims that for the Waiyana the "strict minimum – 4–5 families [16–20 people] – is necessary for mutual aid in cutting fields" (1968:5). However, he notes the existence of villages containing fewer families than four, and he fails to explain why a minimum of four or five men is necessary to cut a field. It is possible that in the past when only stone-axes were available this size of labor force was necessary to cut a field, but the Waiyana have had metal axes for several generations, and it is barely reasonable to explain this minimum in terms of a historical tradition. J.-P. Dumont likewise goes into the question of the minimum size of a Panare village, which, he argues, is controlled by the male mode of work, or more specifically the number of men required to form a collective hunt to spear peccary and tapir; this number is three (1978:72). However, there is nothing intrinsic to the hunting of tapir or peccary that demands the presence of three men, and it is noticeable that such collective hunting is associated with the preparation for rituals.

Although there will be occasion to return to this topic in later chapters, we may note here that there appear to be no technical or ecological factors operating in determining the minimum size of settlements. The question of the maximum size is more problematic. I have argued (1970) that among the Trio the shortage of food, especially meat and fish, gives rise to tensions because social obligations are not fulfilled, and this results in migration by part of the village population. J.-P. Dumont has put forward an argument that relies more directly on the relationship between food shortage and migration. He claims that the maximum size of a settlement is controlled by the mode of production, in which the "variations in the production of big game determine fluctuations in group size" (1978:76). This results from the fact that individual Indians will notice when they have to start doing more work for the same return, and vice versa. In the former case they will move elsewhere and in the latter stay put, although there will be a time lag between changes in productivity and alterations in settlement size.

Dumont's approach is basically a cost-benefit explanation, and a similar position has been adopted by Harris (1979) with reference to the Yạnomamö. The trouble with both Dumont's and Harris's arguments is that they take into account only a single determining factor, big game and animal biomass respectively. Vickers (1980) has argued in favor of a multifactor explanation of settlement patterns, although he still sees the various determinants as ecological in nature. Although I agree that ecological factors must be taken into account, I have yet to see justified the privileged, even unique, position given by certain writers to ecological determinants. The difficulty is that it may not be demonstrable, however good the data, because cost–benefit analysis depends to such a high degree on individual choices and preferences. A relative lack of meat may be more than compensated for by another resource or by the security of close personal relationships. How far does the meat supply have to decline before such relationships begin to appear increasingly less personal and secure?

To argue that all movement of people between settlements or to form new settlements – which is what brings about fluctuations in settlement size – is the result of subsistence needs is wrong, as the ethnography amply demonstrates. The reasons people move are social, political, and ritual as well as economic. The desire to see close kin in another village or the disinclination to stay where one has buried one's child is as strong a motive to move as the wish to eat more meat.

Other questions also arise from the figures presented in the last section. We have noted a more-or-less constant settlement size across the whole region, but there is not a corresponding ecological homogeneity. If the varying conditions all give rise to similar settlement sizes, this is either coincidence or some other factors are involved. Second, if we take an historical perspective we can observe that in the past some of the people had more populous settlements than they have had in recent decades. The decline in settlement size has gone hand in hand with the drop in total population. In ecological terms, two interpretations can be put on this, assuming that the carrying capacity of the environment has not changed. One is that the past population was adapted to the environment and today's is below the carrying capacity of the environment, in which case ecological controls will not be working and cannot account for settlement size. The other is that today's population is adapted to the environment and in the past it was above the carrying capacity of the environment, which raises the question of why ecological controls were not working then.

The obverse to this situation, that in which there has been an increase rather than a decrease in population, is represented by the Pemon. As we have seen, the population has risen sharply, and the number of settlements in the area doubled, but at the same time the size of households and settlements has barely changed at all. Given the relative shortage of forest for garden sites in this savanna environment, it might appear that this is the crucial factor determining settlement size and distribution. This view receives support from Urbina, who claims that it is the ability of local resources to support the population that accounts for the large size of the village he studied. However, he makes no reference to the potential drawing power of the school and church of the Chochiman cult that the village contains (1979:27–9). Thomas also provides evidence that questions the controlling influence of ecological determinants. Garden sites are often located as much as two hours' walk from a settlement (1973:125), and this distance is greater than that between many neighboring settlements (1973:appendix 3). Thomas claims that "dispersion is primarily a fact of social organization rather than of subsistence economics" (1973:125).[8]

That the size of settlements is not entirely the result of ecological determinants is evinced in other ways. Arvelo-Jimenez (1973) has argued that, historically, the size of Ye'cuana settlements fluctuated as a result of hostile incursions into their territory. The Trio missionary villages, which are as much as ten times larger than naturally occurring settlements and have survived for abnormal periods in the same place, continue to exist as much because of the mission personnel's role in settling disputes as anything else. Indeed, it was this ability of external agents to settle disputes and thus maintain the community intact that drew my attention to the sociopolitical factors involved in settlement size. Although the argument will be expanded later, in Chapters 6 and 7, an outline of it may prove useful to the reader at this point.

Throughout the region political authority is weak, and disputes that cannot be resolved are likely to result in the migration of some of the village inhabitants. To some extent, a village's size is an index of its leader's effectiveness, but – however capable he is – the larger the village the more frequent the disputes will be and the less easy to resolve. This is because political relationships are embedded in social relationships, and the density of the latter will be greater in small villages than large ones. Large villages inevitably contain relationships that are intrinsically fragile, and this structural weakness manifests itself in disputes about a range of problems from adultery through food shortages to sorcery and ends in fission.

This summary of an argument to be explored in detail later leads on to a discussion of the pattern of dispersed settlements. Once again there is no intention of denying that ecological factors play a part in determining the separation of villages; but in themselves they cannot account for all the features of this pattern. For example, the defusing of conflict that is achieved through the ready mobility of the population would not work so well if villages were crowded together or further apart. A feature of the settlement pattern that has been noted on several occasions is that the individual village is part of a local group of villages which, as will be shown later, are linked by social, economic, and ritual relationships. The settlement pattern allows both movement from a village, and at the same time the opportunity to remain within the familiar social network. The nature of political institutions, the settlement pattern, and ecological factors form a coherent fit in traditional societies, but it has yet to be demonstrated that the last are the essential determinants. It is right to ask why, if ecological factors determine the nature of the settlement pattern, there exist other institutions that may be understood as functioning to the same end. For example, Butt, having admitted that the movement of the Akawaio is related to the exploitation of subsistence resources, goes on: "As well as this, the social structure and organization heighten the mobility of people and add to the constant shifting from one place of residence to another and back again" (1954:11). Cases in which changes in political organization have resulted in the maintenance of a radically different settlement pattern also throw doubt on whether it is right to endow ecological factors with the prime importance that some writers do.

The question of the duration of villages also deserves to be looked at here, although duration in itself is less interesting than the distance away a new village is built from the old. The reasons for abandoning a village are numerous, and include death, especially of its leader; ineffective leadership; frequency of illness; deterioration of buildings; infestation; increasing distance to garden sites; scarcity of various resources; and hostilities. In many cases, I have noted that a new village is built within the general proximity of the old. Hames (1980) has identified two strategies relating to settlement movement in response to declining game yields. The first, which he calls "pioneering hunting," involves relatively frequent and fairly long-distance moves. The second type, "integral hunting," results in the continuation of the settlement in roughly the same place and the rotation of hunting zones. The latter strategy has been adopted by the Yąnomamö (a Yanoama subgroup) and Ye'cuana among whom Hames worked, and it may well be practiced by other peoples in the area. Certainly more needs to be known about this,[9] although whether the two strategies can account for all cases is, as

*Settlement pattern: size, duration, distribution*

Hames appreciates, questionable. For example, Lapointe states that the average distance between successive sites of Waiyana villages on the Parú is eighteen miles, but that this has nothing to do with the old sites being fished or hunted out (1970:81–2, 85). Other questions that need to be answered are why a population selects one strategy rather than another, the conditions under which a strategy is switched, and whether different strategies may not be employed simultaneously within the same population.

The detailed data on subsistence activities and their returns that exist for some parts of Amazonia are not available for Guiana, although information on these topics has been published by Hurault (1965) for the Waiyana and by Hames (1978, 1980) for the Ye'cuana. This is unfortunate, especially with reference to the subject matter of this chapter, for it is in the settlement pattern that one might expect to see most clearly the influence of ecological factors. Certain points have been made that might indicate, even in the absence of data (and they, as has been said above, may not necessarily provide the answer), that although ecological factors must not be ignored it may be wrong to accept them as the sole determinants. The topics dealt with in the following chapters are those for which it is that much harder to accept an ecological explanation. We turn next to the subject of village composition, and although it is acceptable that ecological factors will play a part in determining the size and distribution of settlements, it is more difficult to argue that they will have a say in who lives with whom or who ought to live with whom.

# 3

# Village composition

Who lives with whom and why, both in fact and thought, and the implications of this, are questions central to the remaining chapters of this study. This chapter forms little more than an introduction to the topic of village composition and deals with the network of social relationships internal to settlements. In Chapters 6 and 7 we will consider the economic, political, and ritual aspects of the subject. This separation into conventional spheres of human social existence is done for expository purposes, and it is appreciated that such a division is often purely arbitrary. Throughout the region decisions on where – or better with whom – to live are informed by social, political, economic, and ritual factors for the simple reason that all these aspects are embedded in a single relationship. Because we have no terms in which to treat such multiplex relationships as though they were single entities, it is necessary to unpack them and deal with them feature by feature. An attempt has been made to alleviate this inevitable dismemberment by gradually reconstituting the parts as the description proceeds. As a result the reader will find some repetition in the following chapters, but this fault seems less than that of leaving unrepaired the fundamental coherence of the relationships involved.

However, even if we choose to ignore the complexity of the relationships that we wish to examine and concentrate solely on a single aspect, in this case that we will refer to loosely as kinship, difficulties remain. In particular, there is the problem of the value of any comparative investigation into the network of existing relationships within villages, even so far as the available data allow this to be undertaken. Given the impermanence of settlements, the mobility of population, the general unpredictability of demographic events, and personal whims, there is likely to be as much variation in the kinship composition of settlements belonging to one group as there is across the whole region. Furthermore, the composition of a single village may change quite radically in a very short time. Thus, from the outset we must be skeptical about whether any useful conclusions can be drawn from the comparison of data on village kinship networks. This is not to say that such information should be ignored, but that for the present we must be satisfied with the general patterns discernible in the material. When the internal political structure of villages is examined in Chapter 6, it will prove important to look more closely at the changing networks of relationships within particular villages; for, as Arvelo-Jimenez has written, "village history is political history" (1973:4).

Alongside this attempt to identify general patterns of social relationships within villages, an account will be taken of the indigenous view of how a village should be constituted socially. To this end, we will be considering native expectations about whom one's co-villagers are or should be, where one should find a spouse, and with whom one should reside after marriage. Although it will quickly become apparent that expressed ideals are rarely attainable or achieved, usually because of the small size of settlements, there is no reason to ignore them because without taking them into account it is that much more difficult, perhaps even impossible, to understand the fundamentals of Guiana social organization. The ideals are a much better guide than the fluctuating networks of relationships, which at any one time only represent futile attempts at fulfilling them.

## II

A start on this investigation may be made with the Ye'cuana, for whom Arvelo-Jimenez (1971) provides a wealth of detailed information. It has already been noted that she associates the size of a village with its stage of development, and we may add here that she further relates it to differences in family structure. Thus she describes a mature village as usually being composed of a single joint household together with several other households. She considers a joint household to be synonymous with a mature extended family, which, in turn, is defined as a family on the threshold of becoming four generations deep. Villages in the incipient and growing stages are normally composed of sets of interrelated household groups, each of which is represented by an incipient extended family of no more than two generations' depth. It would appear that extended families in their initial stage of development consist of little more than nuclear families linked by various combinations of sibling relationships (1971:109–33). This is supported by the fact that for the seven villages for which data are most complete "the core family group . . . had been composed of two or three groups of brothers and sisters whose offspring intermarried as far as possible according to the ideal pattern" (p. 134). This ideal pattern is cross-cousin marriage and uxorilocal residence, together with a strong preference for village endogamy (p. 66).[1] Thus the composition of a village is often either the kindred of an older person or couple, or a group of siblings. However, a village constituted in the former manner can, on the death of the older members, take on the latter form overnight.

The Ye'cuana term for kin is *jöimmä*, and this term may be qualified by *ne'ne*, meaning "real," or by *amöincharotoma*, meaning "close," or left unqualified, in which case it covers all Ye'cuana in contrast with non-Ye'cuana. Both *jöimmä ne'ne* and *jöimmä amöincharotoma* are classed together as *ne'ne*, and in this sense "*ne'ne* corresponds to the category kindred" (1971:169). The relationship between this category of kindred and the actual co-residential group is interesting, as these quotations reveal: "Groups should be based on *ne'ne* relatives" (p. 170); "the ideal is to have a village composed of real *ne'ne* kin" (p. 171). This is rarely achieved, and there will always be more distant kin or strangers present; they are referred to as *jöimmä* (rather than as *ne'ne*). Even so, "village membership is . . . fictionally equated with close kin relationships. . . . Ye'cuana say that fellow villagers are like real close kin. . . . Ye'cuana are very particular about maintaining the belief that a village is a consanguineal unified and solidary whole" (p. 171). Furthermore, it is made clear that at another level of meaning *jöimmä ne'ne* refers to the group of co-residents (p. 181, fn. 8).

This description is of crucial importance; although not always expressed in similar terms or stated quite so explicitly, we will find these ideas and identifications recurring throughout the region. For the next two examples, the Panare and the Piaroa, the evidence is equally clear.

J.-P. Dumont gives the Panare term for members of a co-residential group as *tapatakyen*,[2] of which he writes that "the conscious model . . . is the extended bilateral family of the man who is at the highest genealogical level" (1978:75). He also refers to *pyaka* and states that "an approximate but acceptable rendition of this term is 'kindred,' that is, the ensemble of individuals to whom an individual feels closely related, following the rule of bilateral descent" (1978:76). The actual extension of *pyaka* varies according to individual circumstances. Thus those relatives who are genealogically close but not well known (probably because they live elsewhere) may be excluded in favor of more distantly related but better known people. There is always some overlap between the membership of an individual's *tapatakyen* and *pyaka*, but from what Dumont writes they should ideally coincide exactly.

The description provided by Villalón agrees closely with that of Dumont. "Los residents permanentes de una comunidad son llamados *tapatakien*, mientras que los parientes en particular son designados *piaka*'. Sin embargo, como cada grupo residencial exhibe cierto grado de independencia y endogamia, sucede que muchos de los *tapatakien* son reconocidos como *piaka*'" (1977:747–9).[3] There is no reference to *tapatakyen* in Henley's work, and he contrasts *piyaka* with *tungonan* and glosses the terms respectively as "another of the same kind" and "another of a different kind" (1979:152). He continues: "The specific denotata of these terms varies according to context. Thus in the context of a discussion of residential arrangements, the term *piyaka* is applied by an individual to all those who live in the same settlement whilst the term *tungonan* is applied to those living elsewhere" (1979:152). On the other hand, in the context of kin relations the term *piyaka* refers to close kin. Thus the levels of meaning when combined lead to the situation where "certain Alters whom an individual would regard as *piyaka* on the basis of residence, he will regard as *tungonan* on the basis of the relationship categories" and "the inverse also occurs, that is, those considered as *piyaka* on the basis of relationship may be *tungonan* on the basis of residence" (1979:152–3).

The information from these three Panare ethnographers does not agree exactly. As has been mentioned, Henley makes no reference to the term *tapatakyen*, whereas neither Dumont nor Villalón mentions *tungonan*. For Villalón *piyaka* are kin, for Dumont the bilateral kindred, and for Henley they are kin in the context of the residential group. These differences can almost certainly be explained by the variations that are known to occur between Panare subgroups, but what their exact significance is remains unclear. However, regardless of these differences, what is constant is the fact that the Panare tend to equate the co-residential group with close kin, and in doing this they allow physical proximity to override genealogical distance.

On the question of the actual composition of settlements, the ethnography is uninformative, although Henley identifies three commonly occurring arrangements. The first consists of little more than a nuclear family; the second is an extended family with a man, his wife or wives, unmarried children, and married daughters and their husbands; the third is a group centered on married brothers and sisters, or brothers-in-law. Although it is possible for a settlement to develop through these three stages it is not a necessary progression, and a village may change from any one composition to either of the other two (1979:198–9). The general similarity of this pattern with that described by Arvelo-Jimenez for the Ye'cuana is obvious, the main difference being the absence of nuclear family settlements among the Ye'cuana.

There is agreement about the Panare's preference for local-group endogamy, although, and almost certainly because of the differences in the communities studied, Henley and Dumont disagree on the extent to which this was achieved. Henley, working in a relatively large local group, records a high level of endogamy (1979:172). J.-P. Dumont, on the other hand, notes that local-group endogamy is never achieved; the reason he gives for this is that the ideal of endogamy "conflicts with and contradicts a reverse tendency toward local group exogamy" (1978:82). On demographic grounds alone, the degree of endogamy in the smaller settlement studied by Dumont is likely to be lower, but he argues that the tendency toward exogamy is political in nature and is designed to maintain or set up alliances with neighboring local groups. This topic will be taken up again in Chapter 6, but there are one or two points that deserve to be noted here. It is more important for a small local group to maintain external contacts than it is for a larger, more self-sufficient group. Second, Dumont's informant on this was Marquito who, by Panare standards, was a well-established and relatively powerful leader.[4] It is arguable that the more secure a leader is within his own settlement, the more interested he will be in extending links outside it.

*Individual and society in Guiana*

Finally, on the Panare, there is the question of postmarital residence. Once again statistical data are lacking but there is a consensus about the usual practice. Dumont claims that "the conscious postmarital residence model . . . is uxorilocal" (1978:75), but that this may be only temporary because on completion of bride-service the young couple may choose to take up residence elsewhere. Villalón refers to postmarital residence as being either matrilocal or uxorilocal (it would appear that she is using these terms interchangeably) with isolated cases of virilocality (1977:747). Henley, although declaring there to be "no strict rule of postmarital residence" (1979:152), indicates at various points in his study that uxorilocal residence is common.

Kaplan's study of the Piaroa is focused to a great extent on the questions with which we are here concerned, and the evidence fits well with what we have found to occur among the Ye'cuana and the Panare. The Piaroa term *itso'de* refers both to the house and its inhabitants, in other words the group co-resident in a single settlement. To this must be related the concept *chawaruwang*,[5] which has several levels of meaning. At its widest connotation an individual's *chawaruwang* includes all other Piaroa, and even non-Piaroa with whom one is on friendly terms. Qualified by *tük'ú*, "close," the term refers both to the cognatic kindred as a category and to a particular group within this category who fulfill certain residential and conjugal expectations. The explanation of this is best left in the ethnographers' words:

In its most restricted sense *chawaruwang* is used for the members of a person's immediate kindred, or *tük'ú chawaruwae* ("my close kinsmen"), as opposed to his *otomínae chawaruwae* ("my distant kinsmen"). *Ideally* the former category is comprised of all close genealogical kinsmen (with spouses) related to Ego through both parents extending to the first cousin level and includes, as well, all of the members of Ego's *Itso'de*, or house. Also ideally, the two elements of which this category is comprised – close genealogical relatives and the members of one's house – are isomorphic.
. . . The Piaroa conceive of the house and its inhabitants as a discrete kinship group, one whose membership is based on a principle of consanguinity, or *chawaruwangship*.
. . . The *Itso'de* has a corporate identity which distinguishes it as a group of cognates who live together on a named site, to be contrasted with membership of other houses, each of which is also located on its respective named site. The members of the *Itso'de* espouse the belief, "We are all one, *tük'ú chawaruwang* of one another," that is, a group of consanguineally related and intermarried kinsmen (Kaplan and Kaplan in press:46–8).

This passage has been cited at some length because it is a clear statement not simply of the Piaroa case but also of features that we have noted among the Ye'cuana and the Panare.

Given that the Piaroa see their settlements as inhabited by an endogamous cognatic kindred, and even when it is not behave as though it were, it is not surprising to find that the rule of postmarital residence states that "a young married couple must live with their respective parents" (Kaplan 1975:123). However, if both sets of parents do not live in the same house a choice has to be made. After an initial period of uxorilocal residence, associated with bride-service, the young couple can choose with which set of parents they wish to live (p. 83). When both sets of parents are alive there is a tendency to stay with the wife's (p. 120), and when both sets are dead the stated preference is residence with same-sex siblings, and for a man away from his brothers-in-law (pp. 84–5). However, other factors, such as the desire to live with a powerful leader, may override the expectations about close kin dwelling together (pp. 86–7).

Kaplan makes the point that the choice of where to live, or better with whom to live, is frequently dictated by political considerations. We will be returning to this in Chapter 6, but it is important to reaffirm that politics cannot be divorced from kinship and that together they influence village composition. In larger villages there tends to be a predominance of affinal links and in smaller settlements consanguineal ties. This is well illustrated by the fortunes of the *itso'de* of Sera. As a large village it contained 88 percent of the inhabitants' sibling-in-law relationships and 81 percent of their brother–sister relationships. When the village divided, both these figures dropped to 50 percent, while the figures for parents and married children, and for same-sex siblings living together, remained unaffected (1975:107–9).

Further details indicate other aspects of the Piaroa residence pattern. Although the number of close kin an individual may expect to find in his own house varies between 25 and 90 percent, he can expect more than 90 percent of them to be living in the same territory (*itso'fha*). The percentage of siblings living together varies from 42 for brothers, 50 for brothers and sisters, and 75 for sisters (1975: 120–1). These figures are in line with those reported for the Trio (Rivière 1969a).

As we move on to the savanna to the south and east of those people we have so far been examining, we find that although there is an observable difference in the settlement pattern, there are many similarities in the composition of households and settlements. The best information on the savanna dwellers comes from the Pemon. Among them there is a slight statistical tendency toward uxorilocality across the whole region that is most marked at settlement level but is replaced by a patrilocal trend at zone level (Thomas 1973:129). There is also a large proportion of both men and women living in the same zone as both surviving parent and spouse's surviving parent. This suggests a relatively high degree of zone endogamy, but Thomas argues that such a pattern can also result from the tendency for elderly parents to move in order to live with their children (rather than the other way around). With reference to the question of co-residence among siblings, the figures indicate various features. Siblings do not tend to live in the same settlement, except for sisters who remain living together as a result of the uxorilocal bias. At zone level, the number of sisters present is not much greater than that for brothers and sisters, but a man can only expect to find about 50 percent of his brothers in the same zone. Men who marry out often return to their natal zone at some point, presumably on the death of the wife's parents, and in this way the sibling set may reconstitute itself in old age.

Thomas makes the observation that in any particular case the actual composition of the family will have a bearing on residence. A man who has a sister has a much greater chance of finding a wife locally. Because women are expected to stay at home, and a man with a sister has a much greater chance of staying near home, it is men without sisters who are most likely to have to seek a wife in another zone. This fact has a direct bearing on the statistics that indicate a higher proportion of sisters living together than brothers and sisters or brothers (1973:132–5).

The single explicit rule of residence among the Pemon is that a man must look after his father-in-law, but in practice a number of other variations intervene. For example, it is considered sufficient for only one son-in-law to stay and carry out this duty. The factors that enter into a man's decision to remain in his wife's settlement include the distance from his natal home, the existence of his parents, the amount of work expected of him, and the kind of relationship he has with his in-laws. Indeed the continued presence of in-marrying sons-in-law is crucial if a settlement is to achieve its full cycle of development from nuclear family to three-generation extended family. The size to which any settlement grows depends on this, although polygynous unions and the presence of a married sister and her children play a part. In the end, however, although marriage strategies and sibling ties are vital for building up a large settlement, it is the number of affines that can be held in a settlement that limits its size (1973:144–8, 164).

More recently, Thomas has argued that the "natural" upper limit of a Pemon settlement is six or seven households because it is impossible for a man to maintain ties with his brothers-in-law simultaneously to ties with his sons and sons-in-law. The reasons for this are that affinal obligations bind an individual more closely to his father-in-law than to his brothers-in-law; the ideal of uxori-local residence, which means that a man's sons depart on their marriage; and the fact that relationship between siblings is stronger than that between siblings-in-law (1982:98). He also states that "most decisions about residence are taken with reference to primary relatives" (1982:98).

Although the Pemon material is valuable in providing insights into the factors at work in the constitution of settlements, it is not so clear that there exists the explicit equation, already noted in earlier cases, of close kinship with co-residence, although closeness may be defined spatially or genealogically (Thomas 1978:70). It may be that here where settlements are so small, with nearly half of them consisting of no more than a single household, there is no need to fictionalize the relationship between kinship and co-residence because it is a reality. The same holds true for the preference for settlement endogamy, which can rarely be possible among the Pemon, although Thomas does state that there is "a clear preference for marrying 'close' both spatially and genealogically" (1982:84).[6]

Information from the other savanna-dwelling peoples, the Macusi and Wapishiana, is not good enough to throw any additional light on this. The uxorilocality of the Macusi is agreed upon; some authors describe this as a temporary condition, whereas others imply it is a more permanent state of affairs (Im Thurn 1883:221–2; Farabee 1924:76–7; Myers 1946:26–7; Diniz 1972:82). Farabee (1924:76–7) describes the Macusi as exogamous without explaining to what unit he refers. On the question of who lives with whom the sources are silent, although from Diniz's data (Chapter 4) it can be deduced that there are relatively few three-generation families living together. This may be the result of early death, but it could equally well reflect a tendency for young couples to set up a new domestic group on the birth of children to them.

Data on the Wapishiana are no better. Farabee says they are exogamous, although failing once again to explain what he means by this, and patrilocal, although reference is made to temporary bride-service (1918:93–4). On the other hand, Herrmann notes that the traditional rules involved matrilocality, tribal endogamy, and village exogamy, although the last rule had disappeared completely (1946–7:289).

The quality of the ethnography improves greatly as we return to the forest to look at the Waiwai. Fock (1963:194) reports that the Waiwai village is dominated by a group of siblings and/or parallel cousins; the term for this group is *epeka*. In fact a group of siblings or half-siblings does form the core of the four villages for which data are available (Meggers and Evans 1964). The Waiwai material has been recently submitted to close scrutiny by Morton, and we may refer here to his conclusion that "the main point which is not really brought out with any force in Fock's work is the essentially local importance of the idea of *epeka*, for although siblings who live in other villages must as a question of genealogical necessity be regarded as *epeka*, the relationship is only realised to any extent when siblings are co-resident" (1979:44). There is also the status of "declared *epeka*," and these are unrelated or distantly related individuals who have been adopted as *epeka* as a result of co-residence. We will need to look at the declared *epeka* from a different angle in Chapter 5, but we may agree here with Morton that this manipulation of relationships internal to the village represents "a general effort to give the village an overall structure based on kinship ties, actual and fictitious" (1979:44). This attempt to see or produce a correspondence between kinship, in particular consanguinity, and co-residence is clearly similar to those other cases already described. However, what is different, and it will be necessary to return to this point later, is the emphasis that the Waiwai place on a single generation.

The rule of postmarital residence is described as temporary matrilocality, and Fock claims that "the local group was presumably identical with the matrilocal extended family group, and consequently exogamy was then prevalent; this is still the case in several Waiwai villages, but not in all" (1963:134–5). In other words, in practice Waiwai marriages are the mixture of settlement endogamy and exogamy to be expected. For which arrangement the Waiwai express a preference is not recorded, although Morton has located through his analysis of their myth and ritual certain organizing principles that would suggest a predisposition for endogamy.

It is interesting that whereas Fock represents Waiwai villages as traditionally exogamous, Hurault claims that Waiyana settlements were traditionally endogamous. Although Hurault presents the Waiyana data in a rather inappropriate Africanist terminology, a fairly clear picture emerges. He assumes that there was in the past a form of Waiyana village structure to which all villages complied. It is not clear from where he derives his traditional model of Waiyana village structure, but on the assumption that it was from the Waiyana themselves then presumably he was told by his informants their view of what a village structure ought to be.

The traditional village contained parts of what he calls patrilineages and matrilineages that exchanged women, so that the village was endogamous. However, these lineages do not refer to unilineal descent groups, for the Waiyana "ne considèrent pas matrilignage et patrilignage comme deux groupements distincts: (1968:21).[7] Furthermore, the Waiyana have only a single term for a kin group, *wëuki*, and it seems from Hurault's description that its meaning is similar to, if not identical with, such concepts as *piyaka, chawaruwang*, and *ne'ne*. Although it is not possible to be totally confident about it, the evidence points toward the ideal composition of a Waiyana village as being an endogamous bilateral kindred. Hurault found only one village that fitted this model, and the failure of others to comply he puts down to the collapse of the rule of settlement endogamy. However, it seems no more necessary to attribute it to this than it is to blame, as Fock does, a similar assumed breakdown among the Waiwai for the weakening of the rule of village exogamy.

The actual examples of villages Hurault provides vary widely in their composition. On the question of postmarital residence he notes that in 1964 approximately half the married women with a living father resided with him, whereas the other half lived in their husbands' villages (1968:48). He concludes that the majority of villages consist of a father with some of his married daughters and their husbands, and some married sons with their wives (1968:74).

The Brazilian Waiyana claimed postmarital residence to be matrilocal, but, as Lapointe indicates and as his data confirm, this is by no means the majority practice (1970:71–8). A feature worth noting from both Hurault's and Lapointe's material is the pattern, already met with, of co-resident brothers and sisters, or brothers-in-law.

Among the neighboring Aparaí, the villages are described as consisting of one or two closely related nuclear families. The tendency is toward matrilocal residence, and it is said to be uncommon for daughters to live away from their mothers. However, there are cases of patrilocal residence, and if a women has no daughters she is likely to dwell with a son (Koehn 1975:99). Although no data are provided in support of these assertions, the information fits well with what is reported from elsewhere.

Finally, I would like to refer to the Trio material which, although in line with the evidence presented, requires some recasting, partly in response to critics and partly in the light of additional information from further fieldwork and comparative study.

First, in defining the term *imoitï* I now feel that I overstressed the co-residential aspect of the concept somewhat when I wrote that the "word describes those who live or have lived in the same village over a period time" (1969a:65). The information I collected in 1978 amplified and modified my view. Thus the Trio use the term *imoitï* to refer to all Trio, as opposed to the Waiyana, for example. On the other hand, the term also means close kin, and this is the sense in which the Trio normally understand the word if asked "who are your *imoitï*?" This does not mean that the term lacks the co-residential component previously identified, but that a semantic shift has occurred and the genealogical aspect has become more pronounced. I would argue that this is the result of changes in the settlement pattern, and in particular the formation of large semipermanent villages. Because virtually all kin are now co-resident, the term is used currently to distinguish close kin among all the co-residents rather than to differentiate co-resident kin from those who are not co-resident. I would stand by my earlier claim that "coresidence can be as closely binding as the tie of genealogical connexion, and in Trio thought they are not truly distinguished" (1969a:65). What, however, has happened has been a change of emphasis from co-residence to kinship as a result of altered circumstances. I also suspect that in its most restricted meaning *imoitï* only includes those currently co-resident and not past co-residents, although in a wider connotation it would include them as well. The disruption of the settlement pattern has precluded the possibility of verifying this point.

To sum up the Trio case, the Trio see, by definition, a village as composed of *imoitï*, who, in our terms, constitute a co-resident bilateral kindred, and at the same time the settlement is preferably endogamous. The actual relationships found within a Trio village show a large proportion of brothers and sisters living together, and this accords with the conventional expectation that surrounds this relationship. The high degree of village endogamy is reflected in the large number of an individual's kin and affines who live in the same village. Except for the declared preference for village endogamy (occasional arguments in favor of exogamy are voiced), there is no explicit rule of postmarital residence. There is a tendency toward uxorilocality, but statistically the most frequent arrangement is for married couples to live with surviving parents regardless of whether they are the husband's or the wife's.

At this point we may leave the presentation of ethnography and attempt to delineate the main features of the social composition of settlements within the region. The form itself is clear and varies little, but there are as well the social ideas and practices that underpin and generate the form; these will require closer attention in the remaining chapters.

## III

Although the evidence is not all of the same detail or quality it is remarkably consistent, and the overall picture that emerges is that throughout the region settlements are not simply small (as was demonstrated in the last chapter) but that a quite specific set of ideas is held about their social composition. With certain exceptions, the Pemon and perhaps the Macusi and Wapishiana for whom the evidence is not good enough to know, the societies see the inhabitants of a settlement as being composed of close kin, often a bilateral kindred. This view is strengthened by the failure to make a terminological discrimination between the factors of consanguinity and co-residence; the same term incorporating kinsfolk and co-residents. Nor is this a purely verbal equation, for as I have pointed out for the Trio and Kaplan (1975:123) has echoed for the Piaroa, "co-residence and kinship are not variables."

There is also an almost universal preference for settlement endogamy, which, because of the notion about the social composition of the settlement, implies kindred endogamy as well. Just on demographic grounds it is obvious that none of the people examined is able to practice regularly either kindred or settlement endogamy. The idea that the settlement is inhabited by an endogamous kindred is a fiction that is maintained despite all the evidence to the contrary. This fiction shares in an essential feature of prescriptive alliance in its ability to adjust reality, as necessary and post facto, to fit an ideal form. Just as when, in prescriptive marriage, a union does not conform to the ideal, it is terminologically treated as though it did, so too with "prescriptive endogamy" the social boundaries of the settlement are redrawn as need arises.

Third, there is rarely any explicit rule of postmarital residence, and this fact has to be understood both in the context of the preference for settlement endogamy and the widespread antipathy toward rules. Even so, the distribution of relationships within settlements is not random, and the factors involved in determining where and with whom people live, which are social, affective, political, ritual, and economic in nature, result in a recognizable and repetitive pattern.

Not surprisingly, a fair degree of variation exists in the actual composition of settlements, but it has not been possible to identify a greater difference between peoples than among one people. Accordingly the variation is regarded as the result of contingent factors, whereas the recurring statistical trends in settlement composition are the product of mechanisms and processes general to the whole region. The pattern common to the region involves siblings living together, married couples living with the surviving parent of either spouse, and uxorilocal residence. However, these are not separate and independent arrangements, but a series of interlocking institutions that are often difficult to separate from one another, although a particular people may stress one aspect at the expense of another. For example, uxorilocal residence can equally well result from and be explained by the obligation of the son-in-law to care for his parents-in-law, the close tie between mother and daughter or between sisters, bride-service, and the jural authority a man may exercise over his daughter.

These statistical trends can also be associated in a loose way with different stages in the life cycle of a community, although it is advisable to be cautious about placing too much emphasis on this when considering settlement size and composition. First, there is no necessary lineal relationship between the different stages in the life cycle. Second, the ability of a village to become large or mature is less the result of its age than of its having the right social composition. Thus a co-resident brother and sister, a relatively frequent occurrence, offer considerable potential for growth and durability because around them can develop an endogamous bilateral kindred through the intermarriage of their children. At the same time it is this composition that, under some conditions, seems most vulnerable to fission. Although we will need to return to this point in Chapter 5, it may be indicated here that the presence of the brother–sister relationship entails that of brother-in-law. Which of these two relationships is stressed by any particular people and the actual circumstances of any particular case are variables that cannot be ignored, for they reflect collective ideas about the nature of consanguinity and affinity.

Beyond these commonly recurring patterns of relationship, there usually exists a penumbra of individuals related to the core inhabitants in a variety of ways. It is these people who are likely to represent the most mobile part of the population, and if a generalization can be made it is that the more tenuous an individual's relationship with the core group, the more marginal his position and the less permanent his residence are likely to be. However, two forms of population mobility can be identified. First, there are those continual movements between settlements made by individuals or nuclear families in response to a whole range of reasons: to see kin, to exploit a particular localized resource, to avoid unpleasantness. Second, there are those more major upheavals in which settlements fission, and where the cause is basically political.

Finally, in this chapter, it is useful to make a few comments about uxorilocality to forewarn the reader of an argument developed in Chapter 7. We have noted a stated preference for this form of postmarital residence as well as a statistical trend toward such a practice. Turner (1979) has argued that uxorilocality is the key institution underlying the complex social organizations found among the Gê and Bororo. We return to Turner's argument in Chapter 7 in order to see what there is to be learned from the Central Brazil cases, but it can be noted here that Guiana uxorilocality, despite differences in social organization and the degree to which the practice is followed (these two things are related), does share an essential function with the practice elsewhere. It is the means by which the natal family can retain control over the productive and reproductive capacities of its young women. This crucial point should be kept in mind while we go on to examine the social categories in the idiom of which most relationships are expressed.

41

# 4

# The categories of social classification

In the last chapter it was argued that a common feature of the region is that its various inhabitants maintain the fiction that a settlement is composed of a group of bilaterally related kin. This group often receives verbal recognition although the term involved usually has a broad semantic range, with its meaning dependent upon context in the same way as the English word "family."[1] At the same time the preference for settlement endogamy, together with what has been identified as its prescriptive nature, results in affines also forming part of this co-residential group of kin. This fact fits with the almost total absence of terms to designate a group of affines.

The possible exceptions to this claim are the Waiwai and the Panare. Concerning the former, Fock writes that "an important grouping is the affinal awåle," but because he adds that it also "comprises the more distant relatives" (1963:194), it is probably a mistake to stress the purely affinal nature of this term. It seems probable that *awåle* refers to distantly related, and perhaps unrelated, people, all of whom are potential affines. Among the Panare the term *tunkonan* may in certain contexts mean affines and is "often used as a sort of shorthand for indicating whether someone is marriageable or not" (Henley 1982:101). However, Henley is careful to point out that it would be wrong to regard the terms *piyaka* and *tunkonan* as denoting "discrete classes of 'kin' and 'affines'" (idem.). Furthermore, an individual's *tunkonan* include both related and unrelated people and, according to context, both co-residents and those living elsewhere. The Waiwai case may well be similar, with *epeka* as the opposed term to *awåle*.

The important point is that there do not exist in the region identifiable and enduring groups that can be labeled as kin and affines and that stand in a relationship of spouse exchangers.[2] The closest that one comes to finding such a unit is the nuclear family in which the parents are responsible for seeing that their children obtain spouses. Although this ensures the reproduction of the family and assures the parents of economic security in old age, it is difficult to argue that the family in the region, because of its noncorporate nature, can act as exchange units in the usual sense of the term. Otherwise, groups, insofar as they exist, are ego-centered aggregates of relationships ordered by a set of social categories that is normally referred to as a relationship terminology. The first part of this chapter is devoted to an examination of the salient features of these terminologies, and the second part to the way in which the marriage practices reflect the ordering principles embedded in the terminologies.

# I

An invariant feature of the social organization of the region is that the set of social categories referred to as a relationship terminology is articulated by a principle of prescriptive direct exchange. This does not mean that the terminologies are all identical in the sense that they all contain exactly the same number of terms, and that the genealogical specifications are distributed among the terms in the same way. In fact they are not, and the various terminologies exhibit considerable differences in this matter. Some of these variations are dealt with in this chapter, but others, and specifically those relating to affinity, are left to the following chapter. The point to be stressed immediately is the presence in all the terminologies of the same ordering principles, and it is their generality that justifies the comparison of the differences. The easiest way to handle the discussion is to set out an ideal type against which to assess the variations that occur.

The following description outlines the basic equations and distinctions that are to be found in a simple form of prescriptive direct-exchange terminology. The discussion is cast in terms of genealogical specifications because they constitute a convenient shorthand. However, it must be stressed that there are dangers inherent in this method, for the idiom may be totally alien to the people whose categories we are concerned to understand. The numbers refer to the positions in the accompanying figure, and the convention of using a male ego has been followed.

At ego's own genealogical level the basic features of this type of terminology include one term (5) that covers ego's male siblings and parallel-cousins, a term (7) for female siblings and parallel-cousins, a term (8) for male cross-cousins, and a term (6) for female cross-cousins. The prescriptive and direct-exchange nature of the terminology becomes apparent when we add the affinal specifications. Term 8, that for male cross-cousins, also applies to the sister's husband and wife's brother, and term 6, that for female cross-cousins, to wife, potential wife, and brother's wife.

On the first ascending genealogical level, the important equations are that of father with father's brother and mother's husband (1), and mother with mother's sister and father's wife (2). The significant distinctions are term 1 from term 4, which includes the specifications mother's brother, father's sister's husband, and wife's father, and term 2 from term 3, which covers the father's sister, mother's brother's wife, and wife's mother.

On the first descending genealogical level, the various specifications are ideally distributed among four terms in the following manner: a term (9) for son,

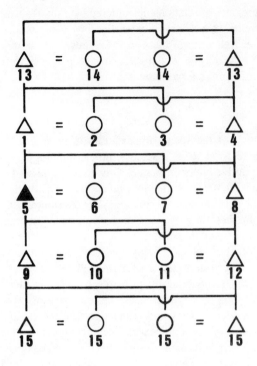

brother's son, male parallel-cousin's son, and female cross-cousin's son; a term (11) for daughter, brother's daughter, male parallel-cousin's daughter, and female cross-cousin's daughter; a term (10) for sister's daughter, female parallel-cousin's daughter, male cross-cousin's daughter, and son's wife; and a term (12) for sister's son, female parallel-cousin's son, male cross-cousin's son, and daughter's husband.

On the second ascending genealogical level, term 13 includes both grandfathers, that is father's father and mother's father, and term 14 both grandmothers, father's mother and mother's mother. On the second descending genealogical level, term 15 covers all the grandchildren.

The principles by which this terminology is ordered are genealogical level; sex; line (transmission); and the relationship of direct exchange, which incorporates the marriage rule. None of the terminologies of the region coincides exactly with this simplified model, but the divergences that occur result from variability in the application of these principles and from the inclusion of age. However, one principle, that of direct exchange, remains constant throughout the region. A possible exception to this claim is the Wapishiana terminology, and a start on the examination of variation may best be made with this case.

It has been suggested (Layrisse and Wilbert 1966:155) that the Wapishiana had adapted their original, either Hawaiian or Eskimo, kinship terminology to the local Carib form to facilitate intermarriage. No evidence is provided in support of this claim. The earliest recorded Wapishiana kin terms are those collected in 1915 by Farabee (1918), and some years ago I undertook an analysis of these (1963:307–11). Although because of certain lacunae in the data it was not possible to be definite, the evidence clearly pointed toward the Wapishiana terminology as being of a prescriptive direct-exchange type. Terms similar to those reported by Farabee were collected by Wirth in the 1930s (see Herrmann 1946–7), and the most recent and complete terminology is that published by Diniz (1968). This last source makes it perfectly clear that the Wapishiana terminology fits the general pattern of the region,[3] and indeed the only major discrepancy from the simplified model described above is that members of the first descending genealogical level are not distinguished by sex. Thus, there is a single term for sons and daughters, and a single term for sister's sons and daughters.

This failure to apply the principle of sex, except at the second descending level, is rare although it is not all that uncommon for the sex of younger siblings to remain terminologically unrecognized. Exceptions to the general rule that sex is not distinguished at the second descending level are the Panare and Piaroa cases. Discussion of the former is best left until a little later, and of the latter it may be noted that what appear to be gender suffixes are a general feature of the terminology.

Age, although of more crucial significance in the governance of the attitudinal and behavioral contents of relationships, also emerges as an ordering principle of the terminologies. The terminological distinction between elder and younger brothers and sisters is very widespread and is usually applied by direct reference to ego. An exception to this is the Aparaí terminology, in which ego classifies his own sibling as older or younger according to their age relative to him or her, but classifies the parallel-cousins according to the age of their parents relative to his or her own parents. Thus the children of father's elder brother are classified as elder siblings by ego regardless of whether they are younger or older (Koehn 1975). Age, together with other criteria, is often the basis for classifying strangers and locating them in an appropriate category. In some terminologies realignment between category and age is simplified by terms that may refer to specifications from more than one genealogical level. This takes different forms and has varying degrees of influence on other features of the terminology.

What appears to be a relatively straightforward example is that of the Piaroa, who use elder-sibling terms for those of the third ascending genealogical level and younger-sibling terms for those of the third descending level (Kaplan 1975:199). More complicated is the Ye'cuana practice. The terms for mother's brother and father's sister are used to refer respectively to the men and women of the third ascending genealogical level. At the same time the terms for sister's son and sister's daughter are used for men and women respectively of the third descending level. A male ego refers to a classificatory grandfather of similar age to himself by the term for male cross-cousin and to a classificatory grandmother of similar age to himself by the term for woman of the same genealogical level as himself. Consistent with this is the usage whereby a classificatory grandchild of the same age as ego "is treated like a cross-cousin and is addressed accordingly" (Arvelo-Jimenez 1971:155).

The Panare terminology provides a variation on this pattern. It is the only terminology in the region to have four terms for grandparents, distinguishing them not only by sex but also by line. There are also four terms for the second descending genealogical level, and these reflect clearly the importance of alternation in the ordering of the terminology. Thus a male ego's son's children are referred to by the same terms as ego uses for his brothers and sisters, whereas his daughter's children are referred to by the same terms as he uses for wife and male cross-cousins according to sex. At the same time a female ego refers to her mother's father by the same term she uses for her husband. Thus those who stand in the relationship of mother's father and daughter's daughter to one another also stand in the relationship of husband and wife. This reflects the Panare view that marriage between such members of alternate genealogical levels is particularly suitable (Henley 1982:90–1, 98–100).

Although in these cases there is terminological equation of specifications from alternate genealogical levels, the Trio terminology contains terms drawing their specifications from adjacent levels. Thus the patrilateral cross-cousins, the mother and mother's brother, are covered by two terms (sex specific), and similarly the matrilateral cross-cousins and the sister's children.

The presence of terms that cover specifications from more than one genealogical level is more than just a mechanism for realigning age with category. It allows for considerable manipulation of the terminology, and this is further enhanced by the absence of any formal groupings and by the fact that relationships may be traced equally through men or women. Given the fluidity of relationships in the region, it is not surprising that the relationship terminologies exhibit a similar quality. A particular advantage that this flexibility allows is the widening of marital possibilities by reclassification as marriageable.

The Trio terminology also contains some other problematic features. For example, at the first descending genealogical level no distinction is made between brother's children and sister's children, or, in other words, the "lines" merge. This, however, is merely a terminological difficulty that causes no problems in practice because the relationship can always be specified by reference to the parental generation. Thus a man instead of saying "he is my sister's son" will turn the statement into "I am his mother's brother" (Rivière 1969a:69).

This merging of lines also apparently occurs in the terminologies of the Aparaí, Ye'cuana, and Pemon at ego's own genealogical level. Thus there are distinct terms for same-sex siblings and same-sex cross-cousins, but only a single term to cover all members of the opposite sex (Koehn 1975: 84–5; Arvelo-

*Categories of social classification*

Jimenez 1971:150–5; Thomas 1978:73–4).[4] In practice this terminological equation of the marriageable and the unmarriageable causes no confusion. The apparent difficulty is dealt with by reference to the first ascending level. The marriageable individual is identified as a father's sister's or mother's brother's child, which is the form of words in which the marriage prescription is anyhow normally expressed, as we shall see below. The distinction between marriageable and unmarriageable members of the category may also emerge in behavioral differences, but this is a matter best left until the nature of affinity is examined in the next chapter. This is also true of a singular feature of the Waiwai terminology, in which the cross-cousins, for which distinct terms exist, may also be classified as siblings (Fock 1963:187–9).

So far we have concentrated on these terminologies as sets of classificatory terms, but many of them contain descriptive terms whose referent is a single consanguineally or affinally defined individual. This occurs relatively infrequently with regard to consanguines and where it does it exclusively concerns the parent–child relationship. The cases are the Waiyana, who have terms that distinguish both father and son (Lapointe 1970:109–10); the Aparaí, with a distinct term for just the father (Koehn 1975:84–5); the Akawaio, with father and mother terms (Colson, personal communication); and the Barama River Caribs, with father, mother, son, and daughter terms (Adams 1972:128–33). It is difficult to identify any particular pattern in these cases either with reference to the internal arrangements of the people concerned or in comparison with one another. Adams (1972:128–33; see also 1979) argues that these terms, not reported by Gillin thirty years before, are innovations resulting from changed economic circumstances that, in turn, have tended to isolate the nuclear family. Although this explanation may well be right with regard to the Barama River Caribs, it does not necessarily apply elsewhere. Indeed, throughout the region, the nuclear family is the significant productive and reproductive unit regardless of whether its internal relationships receive special terminological recognition.

The occurrence of distinct terms for husband and wife is widespread, and there are few terminologies that fail to pick out the marital relationship by either distinct reference terms, direct address terms, or both. However, of greater sociological interest are the affinal terms, and these deserve some extended attention. From one society to another there is variation in the number and distribution of such terms, and in the degree to which they are purely affinal in nature.

At one extreme are such groups as the Waiyana, Macusi, and Akawaio, whose terminologies contain no purely affinal terms, in the sense that there are no terms that refer to affines that are distinct from those referring to consanguines. Thus, in these terminologies, the mother's brother is equated terminologically with the father-in-law, the wife's mother with the father's sister, the male cross-cousins with the brothers-in-law, the sister's son with the son-in-law, and the sister's daughter with the daughter-in-law. It would appear that the Pemon also belong with this group, for although they possess two distinct terms, one for the spouse's mother and the other for son-in-law, Thomas notes that they are "in practice, subsumed under consanguineal terminology" (1973:92).

At the other extreme is the terminology in which all affinal positions have distinct terms, lacking in any consanguineal specification. The unique example of this appears to be the Trio terminology, which contains a separate term for each of the following affines: father-in-law, mother-in-law, brothers-in-law, son-in-law, and daughter-in-law.

There are also two other possibilities. First, there is the terminology that contains distinct terms for those from adjacent genealogical levels; in other words, for father-in-law, mother-in-law, son-in-law, and daughter-in-law, but none for those of ego's own level, the brothers-in-law. The Ye'cuana represent an example of this possibility. The other possibility is one in which there are purely affinal terms for those of ego's own genealogical level, but none for affines of adjacent levels. There does not appear to be a clear-cut case of this, but the Panare terminology comes closest to it. Their term *tamun* certainly means brother-in-law, but it is used interchangeably with another term, *pamo*, to address and refer to classificatory and potential brothers-in-law. *Tamun* is used when the speaker wishes to stress the closeness of the relationship. The *tamun* relationship is characterized by intimacy and generosity and is thus a marked relationship among the affinal relationships (Henley 1982:99).

A further form that occurs is that in which the affinal terms, although distinct from kin terms, are created by combinations of kin terms. The Piaroa terminology contains this feature, and Kaplan refers to it as a system of teknonymy. Thus the spouse's father becomes the "grandfather of my child," and the kin link is stressed at the expense of affinal relationship. Not all Piaroa affinal positions are expressible in this way, since, as Kaplan notes, in the case of brothers-in-law it is not possible to do this (1975:172–4). A similar system of affinal nomenclature is to be found among the Barama River and Maroni River Caribs, and possibly among the Aparaí. This last case is a little obscure, although the parents-in-law terms are constructed around the grandparent terms and the children-in-law terms appear to contain the root that occurs in the terms for grandchildren and sister's children (Koehn 1975:84–6).

For the present, the intention is only to note that variations in the nature and distribution of kin and affinal terms. The significance of the differences and similarities will become apparent only when, in the next chapter, the terminologies are reunited with their attitudinal and ideological correlates. The importance of doing this is well illustrated by a case that has received little attention so far, that of the Waiwai, whose terminology is particularly difficult to understand outside its social context. First, however, rather more detailed attention needs to be paid to marriage rules and practices.

## II

In dealing with the subject of marriage, it is unrealistic to separate the genealogical aspect from the residential component, for as has been observed in the last chapter the factor of kinship is not easily distinguished from that of co-residence. It was argued there that the preference for settlement endogamy is part of the view of the community as a self-contained body of kinsfolk. This fiction or idealization of the nature of the settlement is helped by what we have termed "prescriptive endogamy." This institution, operating in a manner similar to an essential aspect of a prescriptive terminology, ensures, post facto, that whatever happens is reinterpreted in terms of what should happen. At a linguistic level, the fiction is not difficult to maintain because of the terminological equation of co-residents and kinsfolk. In practice, however, it is not so easy, especially when the settlement grows beyond a critical size and the harmony and stability of the kin group are threatened by the incorporation of too many outsiders. This is a crucial matter to which we will need to devote greater attention in Chapter 6. Another point to which we will also return is that, although the emphasis so far has been placed on the preference for settlement endogamy, the advantages of settlement exogamy are often recognized.

In more purely kinship terms, we may repeat that in all the groups with which we are concerned the prescribed category includes the genealogical specifications of the bilateral cross-cousin. The prescribed category also covers classificatory cross-cousins and may also be applied to distantly related or unrelated people. In some cases the prescribed category draws its genealogical specifications only from ego's own genealogical level, whereas in others it includes specifications from more than one level; from adjacent levels in mother's brother–sister's daughter marriage, and from alternate levels where grandparents and grandchildren are involved. This extension of the prescribed category I have suggested is a device for increasing the pool of potential spouses. However, the marriageability of those from other genealogical levels is often circumscribed by age. Thus a Ye'cuana classifies as cross-cousins only those from the second ascending and descending genealogical levels who are of similar age. Data on the relative age of spouses are scarce, but the general impression is that the age gap between husbands and wives is not great (under eight years in the majority of cases among the Trio and under five among the Pemon) and that husbands are more often than not older than their wives. This does not mean that there are not numerous examples of men who have married much younger girls, usually as a second wife, nor of the less frequent occurrence of young men married to women of their mother's age.

The way in which the anthropologist perceives the marriage rules, in particular in his perception of them as embedded in the terminology itself, differs from the way in which the Amerindians express their rules. More often than not they do this by reference to the offspring of a category rather than the prescribed category itself. One reason for this, and others will be given below, is that to state the rule in terms of the prescribed category is in some instances to render it vacuous. Thus for a Trio to say he should marry an *emerimpë* is to say no more than that he should marry someone who is marriageable. Instead the Trio state their rule in terms of marrying a child of a *nosi*, a category that includes the father's sister and women of the second ascending genealogical level. The Pemon enjoin marriage with a *wa?nɨ-mure*, the child of a *wa?nɨ* or a father's sister (Thomas 1973:156). The Panare express their rule in terms of marriage with a *wa'nyenkin*, a child of a *wa'nyene*, which category includes the father's sister as well as the daughter of an opposite-sex sibling (Henley 1979:150).

These examples emphasize the patrilateral aspect, but this cannot be regarded as significant in any way. This is partly because in most cases there is an equal awareness, if not expression, of the appropriateness of marrying the matrilateral cross-cousin, and partly because the direct-exchange element involved in patrilateral cross-cousin marriage is stated more explicitly in other ways; for example, as sister exchange. Given the structure of the relationship terminologies, it is no surprise to find such exchanges occurring, but Kaplan has warned that it may be wrong to give too much emphasis to such arrangements. Among the Piaroa she claims that sister exchange is more appropriately labeled the "serial exchange of children by two affines" (1975:135), which better fits with their own description of a proper marriage as being one in which the spouses' fathers are brothers-in-law (1975:133).

Henley has further broken down this notion, which he has retermed "serial affinity." The Panare are concerned to "marry someone from a conjugal family to which their own conjugal family is already connected by marriage," and Henley distinguishes three forms of serial affinity: in a single generation by intermarriage between two sibling sets; in the succeeding generation by cross-cousin marriage; and in the second descending generation by marriage with a daughter's daughter (1982:109). He further points out that within a single generation there are two distinct forms of serial affinity, what he calls "reciprocation" and "replication." Reciprocation applies to sister exchange, and replication refers to such unions as sororal polygyny or a set of brothers marrying a set of sisters. Kaplan (1981:163) has argued that within an endogamous community there is no need to distinguish between reciprocation and replication because they are both aspects of a generalized exchange through which "the very notion of marriage exchange . . . [is] erased." However, the context and entailments of reciprocation and replication are by no means identical, and much depends on the specific social and political circumstances.

To close this chapter, we will turn from the rules relating to marriage and look at marriage practices. There are some fundamental difficulties in interpreting the figures that exist. For example, given the high rate of population mobility and the impermanence of settlements, any attempt to compute the extent of settlement endogamy is problematic. The only measure of endogamy, which is far from satisfactory, is the degree to which married couples reside with the kin of both spouses. Bearing such difficulties in mind, the information relating to endogamy and the relatedness of spouses will be reviewed briefly.

Among the Trio it is possible to trace some form of relationship between 18 percent of the married couples. This figure is probably too low as a result of gaps in the genealogical information. Various pieces of evidence can be marshaled to support this claim. The first has to do with the density of relatedness. An average Trio can expect to find 69 percent of closest kin and affines as co-residents, 80 percent of them within the same cluster of villages. With such figures one might expect to have found more genealogically related spouses,[5] and that the failure to do so is the result of genealogical amnesia was brought home by the number of second-cousin marriages recorded in 1978. The nature of these unions was only identifiable because of the genealogical depth contained in the ethnographer's notebooks.

The Piaroa statistics match those of the Trio very closely. Kaplan records considerable variation between *itso'de* (25 to 90 percent), but more than 90 percent of an individual's close kin are to be found within the same *itso'fha* (1975:120). The number of marriages between those with traceable genealogical connections is described as very few (1975:140).

The Pemon exhibit a much higher proportion of marriages between those genealogically related. Thomas gives an overall figure of 35 percent (1973:152), and he also provides information on regional and zonal endogamy. The figure for regional endogamy is 61 percent, and some interesting variation occurs in zonal endogamy. The zones with the highest rate of endogamy (around 40 percent) are those with the largest populations and a relatively high proportion of genealogically related spouses. However, figures from other zones show that there is no obvious correlation between a zone's size of population, number of genealogically related marriages, and rate of endogamy. Thus the two smallest zones have the highest rates of genealogically related marriages but no cases of zone endogamy (1973:153–4). The size and composition of a particular population are vital factors when it comes to finding an appropriate spouse near to home, as the following case studies further illustrate.

Henley admits that it is difficult to provide "any statistical measure of the degree of local endogamy in Panare society on account of the impermanence and fluidity of Panare settlement groups" (1979:172). He does point out that the recent influx of people into the area in which he worked has increased the chance of finding a spouse locally and out of 26 unions involving men under 30 years old only 3 had come from outside the valley (1979:172). On the question of the incidence of marriage between genealogically related individuals he has some particularly pertinent observations, based on his fieldwork data, to make. First he notes that out of the 54 unions in his fieldwork sample, 12 (or 22 percent), are between people who are genealogical cross-cousins to one another. All these 12 cases involve men under the age of 30, and because there are only 26 such marriages, the proportion of cross-cousin marriages rises to 46 percent in the 15–29 age cohort. This concentration can be explained in two ways. First, that it is only an "apparent concentration" and a similar proportion may occur in the older generation but it is not possible to collect the genealogical information necessary to demonstrate it. Second, there is a demographic factor to account for a genuine concentration. The high rate of cross-cousin marriages results from the fact that two generations ago a man had 19 children by 3 different wives. These children provided him with 81 grandchildren, 76 of whom, equally divided between the sexes, still live in the area. Thirty-nine of these individuals have married, and the intermarriage of 22 of them accounts for 11 out of the 12 cross-cousin unions referred to above (1979:182–4).

The Ye'cuana information fits into the general picture that is emerging. According to Arvelo-Jimenez's Table 8 (1971:138), there are 114 current marriages. Of these, 28 are between closely related cross-cousins, 12 between distant cross-cousins, 5 between closely related members of alternate genealogical levels (grandparent/grandchild), and 6 between distantly related members of these levels.[6] If we exclude the distant relations, then 29 percent of the unions are between closely related people; and if we include the more distant relatives, then 45 percent of the marriages are between people who are genealogically related in some way.

Figures on local or settlement endogamy are more difficult to compute from Arvelo-Jimenez's material, but it would appear from her Table 6 (1971:115–16) that out of a total of 145 unions 93, or 64 percent, are endogamous. However, if we compare Tables 6 and 8 we can see once again that there is no obvious correlation between settlement size, settlement endogamy, and the proportion of marriages between genealogically related individuals. The largest village has a high rate of endogamy but a rather low proportion of marriages between genealogically related individuals. If we discount this case, and it is legitimate to do so because the presence of a mission station has artificially inflated its size, then the next largest villages are those containing 10 to 12 married couples and are characterized by equally high proportions of endogamy and genealogically related marriages. It is villages of this sort that Arvelo-Jimenez describes as "consolidated" or "mature"; she writes of them: "Residence within a large group of kinsfolk is advantageous with respect to marriage. The larger the group of close relatives the greater one's chances are of finding a proper marriage partner (a true or classificatory cross-cousin) within one's natal village" (1971:66). Although this statement, that larger the settlement the greater the chance of finding an appropriate spouse, is broadly true, it overlooks the problem of how and why the settlement survived into maturity. Here it is the composition of the relationships within the settlement that is crucial. To understand this it is necessary first to examine the nature of interpersonal relationships, and in particular their political content. The initial step in this direction is taken in the next chapter, but to conclude this chapter there is one further matter that deserves our attention.

In this last section we have been looking at, among other things, the extent to which marriage rules, prescriptive and preferential, are followed. This has been done in genealogical terms, and for reasons given (demographic impossibility and genealogical ignorance) the actual proportion of marriages between individuals in the correct genealogical relationship is nowhere very high. However, it must be stated that in using a genealogical criterion we are misrepresenting the situation, because the Indians express relationships in categorical rather than genealogical terms. This is apparent in the conceptual blurring that occurs between kinship and co-residence. Furthermore, if we look at the relationship between spouses in terms of their category membership rather than their genealogical connection, we find a very high proportion of marriages are between correctly related individuals; in other words, between members of the prescribed categories (see Kaplan 1975:135–40; Rivière 1969:143–8).

This emphasis on category does not imply that the Indians are unaware of genealogical relationships, and in practice it is not easy to make a clear-cut distinction between genealogy and category. Among Guiana Indians, an individual's social network is small, and the chances are that everyone in it is genealogically related in some way and often in more than one way. Daily interaction occurs between people who, if not consanguineally or affinally related, treat each other as though they were. The classificatory terminology helps achieve this, allows the integration of co-residential qualifications with those deriving from kinship, and provides a framework of social roles that are simultaneously categorical and individual.

It is important to understand this not only for our assessment of marriage practices but also for our appreciation of everyday life within the confines of a single community. In the next chapter, where we examine conventional attitudes and behaviors, the distinction between biological and classificatory members of a social category may be ignored as irrelevant in the village setting.

# 5

# Aspects of social relationships

In the last chapter we were concerned with the classification of people and with the rules including those relating to marriage, that underlie it. Here we attempt to flesh out these terminologies and rules and to understand what they mean in the interaction of everyday life. In doing so we must remember that the social circles in which daily transactions take place are extremely small, and contain, if not always in practice at least notionally, closely related individuals. We will initially go along with this fiction, but later in the chapter it will be necessary to examine how increasing physical and social distance (insofar as they are separable) influences the contents of the various relationships.

In the inspection of the relationship terminologies certain features emerged as important in their ordering. These were genealogical level, relative age, sex, and affinity. For the purpose of this present chapter it is initially necessary to break down the last feature into four analytically distinguishable relationships: marital, marriageability, affinity, and affinability. Definitions of these terms will be provided at the appropriate places in the text.

In the first part of this chapter we will examine the behavioral correlates of age, sex, and genealogical level; in the second part the focus is on affinity and its four distinguishable aspects; and in the third part some general remarks are made about the nature of affinity in the region.

## I

Genealogical level operates as an ordering principle in all the relationship terminologies, as does relative age. So far we have only described how the latter factor is employed in the distinction of elder from younger siblings, but in practice it has a more far-reaching influence, especially when we turn from the criteria that define the terminological categories to the content of the relationship between them. Where genealogical level and age difference accord, as, for example, in the case of mother and son, it is safe to argue that it is genealogy that determines the categorical relationship. Indeed, an ideal model of conventional attitudes and behaviors, which would assume the congruence of genealogy and

54

age throughout the system, would suggest that genealogy is generally the determining factor. In fact, however, this argument only applies among closely related people, and among more distantly related individuals it is their relative age that is significant. Among the Pemon, Thomas found an increasing use of relative age in the classification of individuals as they became genealogically and residentially more remote from the informant (1973:102). This would also be an appropriate conclusion to draw from the material on the Trio, among whom genealogy is the more important classificatory principle for those more closely related and age the more important for those categories into which strangers are more likely to be placed (Rivière 1969a:80–3). The Ye'cuana provide a further example of the use of age in their practice of reclassifying as cross-cousins classificatory grandparents/grandchildren of similar age.

Where genealogical level and age difference do not properly coincide, it may be possible to manipulate the categories so they do. In this way relative age often determines the categorical relationship and brings about the congruence of genealogy and age, on which alignment the model of conventional behaviors and attitudes is based. Thus it may be broadly true to say that although the relationship between categories is specifiable in genealogical terms, the content of the relationship is highly dependent on the relative age of those involved, and any serious discrepancy leads to reclassification. Therefore, it is appropriate to place emphasis on the factor of age. However, it ought not to be overlooked that within the narrow confines of the village and given the numerous genealogical links between the inhabitants, serious discrepancy between genealogy and age is not a frequent occurrence.

Throughout the region, the conventional attitude of the young toward the old, and of members of a junior genealogical level toward those of a senior level, is one of respect, although this may be tempered by other attributes. Thus an attitude of respect does not exclude the closeness of a mother–child relationship. But, at the same time, the point in the life cycles of those involved needs to be taken into account. It is generally true to say that the rules and conventions that guide behavior and attitudes are only fully applicable to those of full adult status; those who exemplify full male and female potential and capacities. The rules are relaxed for the immature, as Arvelo-Jimenez (1971:163) notes when she writes "when one of the people in the pair is a child avoidance does not apply." And to some extent this is equally true of the very old. Thus the warm and close relationship with a parent experienced by the young child may develop into a more austere and reserved relationship as the latter grows up. Likewise the free and easy relationship often reported to exist between those of alternate generations, between grandparents and grandchildren, is not likely, given the life expectancy in the region, to involve adults.

Difference of sex is a fundamental feature of the social, economic, political, and ritual organizations of all the societies in the region. The activities of men and women in these spheres are distinct, but at the same time complementary.

The relationship terminologies faithfully reflect this importance, and sex difference is a central ordering principle of all terminologies. Sex difference is also a crucial determinant of conventional attitudes and behaviors. Broadly speaking, the relationship between those of the same sex is egalitarian, whereas that between those of the opposite sex is asymmetrical, with women in the subordinate position. However, in both cases the nature of the relationship is modified by age difference. Thus the equality of the same-sex, same-age relationship becomes modified and more unequal with increasing age difference. In the case of the opposite-sex relationship, if the man is older than the woman the asymmetry is merely confirmed, but when the woman is older than the man the relationship may be inverted.

In rather general terms, relationships between members of the opposite sex tend to be marked by restraint, and relationships between those of the same sex by closeness. However, once again age modifies this pattern so that restraint tends to be intensified and closeness diminished with increasing age difference. However, this simple picture of conventional attitudes and behaviors ordered along lines of absolute similarity or difference in sex and variable difference in age is vastly complicated by the presence of three other factors; they are marriageability, affinity, and affinability. In the next section I will explain briefly what I mean by these terms, and then turn to ethnographic examples to demonstrate how they, together with age and sex, produce varying patterns of interpersonal relationships.

## II

The quality of marriageability is by definition a feature only of relationships between those of the opposite sex, and as such is distinct from affinability, which occurs in both same-sex and opposite-sex relationships. Marriageability, as the term suggests, denotes a relationship of potential marriage, and may accordingly exist between related individuals of the appropriate categories and unrelated people.

The term "affinability" refers to the potential for becoming an affine, whereas the word "affinity" will be reserved for the relationships between an individual and his or her spouse's closest kin. We have seen in the last chapter that all the terminologies contain the notion of affinability, for they all have categories whose specifications are both consanguineal and affinal. However, not all terminologies mark affinity, in the sense of containing distinct affinal terms, and those that do, do so in a variable fashion.[1]

To these terms, I would like to add a further distinction, which I found useful in my analysis of Trio affinity (1969a:ch. 9); it is that between related and unrelated affines. Related affines are those linked by consanguinity and/or co-residence prior to the marriage that brought affinity into existence, whereas the latter are those unrelated prior to the union. It is not implied that there are two classes of affines, but rather that there are fine gradations between two extreme types, and that the forms of attitudes and behaviors vary depending where on this continuum between related and unrelated any particular individual stands. The unrelated in-marrying spouse, conventionally and usually a man, has to practice almost total avoidance and submit to the full obligations of bride-service. On the other hand, the related affine experiences little change in attitudes to those prevailing before marriage, and the requirements of bride-service represent little more than the expected forms of cooperation between kin. The difference in the relationship between kin and that between unrelated affines may be summed up in the differences between cooperation and obligation and between respect and avoidance.

It is not proposed that the distinctions between related/unrelated and affinability/affinity that are so pronounced in the Trio case are applied with the same degree of intensity everywhere or even elsewhere. However, it is worth examining the Trio case in a little more detail because it does represent one end of the spectrum.

The Trio, as was noted in Chapter 4, are exceptional in the region in having distinct terms for all affinal positions. Furthermore, the affinal terms are reference terms only and lack an address form, unless one existed prior to marriage as would be the case for related affines. This correlates with the fact that unrelated affines avoid one another and do not talk to each other, whereas only respect is enjoined on related affines. The Trio have words for these different forms of behavior and are perfectly explicit about their application. A man respects other men older than himself, women, and related affines; jokes with men of similar age and marriageable women; and avoids unrelated affines. Sex, age, marriageability, and affinity all have implications for modes of behavior, but affinability does not unless it concerns a stranger. The relationship between a man and his father is no different from that between him and his mother's brother, his potential father-in-law. If this potential is realized, then the fact of affinity does increase the distance between the two men, but not to the point where avoidance is practiced.

The particular features of the Trio case take on greater significance in comparison with other examples, although the number of these with detail enough to make comparison feasible is limited. Fortunately, one of the fullest accounts is that for the Pemon, whose relationship terminology, in contrast to that of the Trio, is virtually devoid of separate affinal terms. Two only exist, that for mother-in-law and that for son-in-law, but Thomas remarks that they "are, in practice, subsumed under consanguineal terminology" (1973:92) and rarely used (1973:98). However, it is worth stressing that the terms that do exist mark the relationship that is most likely to be characterized by distance and constraint.

Thomas considers the dyadic relationships contained in the terminology and describes the conventional attitudes associated with them (1973:94–7). We will summarize these.

The relationship between grandparents and grandchildren is one of familiarity and affection, with respect but no deference for the senior generation by the junior.

Deep and lasting affection characterizes the relationship between parents and children of both sexes.

The relationships between mother's brother and sister's children, and father's sister and brother's children, involve "both affinal and consanguineal ties and hence carry the connotation of a rather guarded closeness, a sense of obligation underlying the mantle of kindred solidarity. . . . The relationships imply a certain distance, even in their consanguineal usage. The MB/ZS [mother's brother/sister's son] relation is among these relationships, though no particular set of obligations or deferential behaviours characterizes that relationship. Though MB is a wife-provider . . . no special attitudes, other than that of respect and a certain social distance, characterize these relations before marriage."

It is also worth citing at length Thomas's description of the nature of the relationship between same-sex cross-cousins. They are "affinal in tone, connoting obligation, an obligation expressed in terms of direct (equivalent) reciprocity. Even the consanguineals subsumed under these terms take on an affinal cast, and though the sense of obligation is diminished if affinal and consanguineal bonds coincide, the dominant motif is one of obligation. Pemon tales are replete with hostile tricks played by affines on one another[2] . . . and an element of competition or friction underlies these relationships. Those with whom one is involved in sister-exchange, even though they be consanguineals, are in some sense suspect and yet are obliged to keep the peace."

Between same-sex siblings and parallel-cousins there is familiarity, closeness, and cooperation free of competition. Within the nuclear family the relationship between brothers and sisters is just as strong as that between siblings of the same sex. However, for others standing in the relationship of brother and sister there is a "certain middle range of social distance," and the "junior-senior differentiation is more strongly accentuated in the cross-sex than in the same-sex ties." The junior shows respect for the senior and receives affection in return.

In his recent monograph (too recent unfortunately to be able to take full account of it), Thomas has presented this information in tabular form (1982:72) and distinguishes between three basic forms of relationship: siblingship, filiation, and affinity. Later in the same work he expresses this in a rather different way (1982:233) when he distinguishes between two forms of hierarchy and one of reciprocity. What he refers to as the "hierarchy of responsibility" characterizes the relationship between parents and child, older and younger siblings. On the other hand, the "hierarchy of demands" is a quality of the relationship between parents-in-law and son-in-law, and of leaders and shamans who abuse their position. Meanwhile, direct reciprocity marks the relationship between unrelated people of similar age, affines of similar age, and the proper behavior of leaders and shamans.

Although this looks relatively straightforward, there is here the difficulty already noted that the terms for elder and younger siblings of the opposite sex also cover the opposite-sex cross-cousins. Thomas likens the elder brother–younger sister relationship to that between husband and wife, whereas toward an elder sister (and an elder female cross-cousin is not marriageable) a man will have "quasi-maternal sentiments" (1978:74–5). However, this is further complicated by the fact that Thomas argues that social distance from ego increases through same-sex siblings, opposite-sex siblings, same-sex cross-cousins to opposite-sex cross-cousins. The criteria involved are a combination of sex difference and affinability. The absence of a term for opposite-sex cross-cousins means that "a category expressing maximum social distance has been suppressed" (1978:76). It will be necessary to return to this point later in this chapter in order to discuss the conclusions that Thomas draws from this, but for the present a number of points may be noted. First, no argument is made for characterizing the relationship between those who are marriageable as affinable. Second, it has been observed above that far from suppressing what is usually the most distant of affinal relations, that between mother-in-law and son-in-law, the Pemon mark it with special terms. Third, it is not clear that the Pemon lack a term for opposite-sex cross-cousin. Thomas (1978:73) correctly translate *na?nai* as own-generation elder female for a male ego, but in the course of the argument *na?nai* becomes elder sister without the case for such a shift being made. Finally, we are not informed whether the relationship between brothers and sisters and that between opposite-sex cross-cousins is the same because, as we will see, there is no reason why members of the same categories should not be differentiated in terms of attitudes and behaviors.

This problem apart, which appears effectively to exclude marriageability as a distinct form of relationship, the Pemon case provides interesting parallels and instructive contrasts with that of the Trio. In both societies age and sex play an equally important and not dissimilar part in determining behavioral and attitudinal expectations. Second, the difference in conventional behavior between kin and between affines is similar; the former relationships are marked by closeness and cooperation, the latter by restraint and obligation. Third, although affinability is a more pronounced feature among the Pemon than it is among the Trio, the difference between affinability and affinity is not clear-cut among the former. Thus the relationships between parents-in-law and children-in-law "are not characterized by any formal avoidance or special deferential behaviors" (1973: 123). This fits with the fact that there is no qualitative difference between related and unrelated affines (the sense of obligation is described merely as being diminished when consanguineal and affinal ties coincide), and with the virtual absence of any separate terms for affines.

We may now turn from the Pemon to the Ye'cuana who, although sharing certain terminological features, at the same time differ in others. Like the Pemon, the Ye'cuana classify together opposite-sex siblings and opposite-sex cross-cousins, but unlike them their terminology does contain separate parent-in-law and children-in-law terms, although not a brother-in-law term. Arvelo-Jimenez notes that the content of the relationship between kin (*ne'ne*) is similar to that between affines and involves economic and technical cooperation and political support. She also identifies four forms of behavior, each of which characterizes a particular set of categorical relationships. There is some question concerning the status of these behavioral forms because it is not clear whether the Ye'cuana themselves distinguish them. These forms are unrestrained joking, restrained joking, unrestrained authority, and restrained authority. These will be dealt with in turn (see Arvelo-Jimenez 1971:159–64).

Unrestrained joking takes place with those of the same sex who are cross-cousins or classificatory siblings of similar age, between spouses and with a spouse's same-sex siblings.[3]

Restrained joking occurs between opposite-sex cross-cousins.

Unrestrained authority is an aspect of the relationships between child and same-sex parent, grandchild and same-sex grandparent, and elder and younger same-sex siblings.

Restrained authority operates between a child and the opposite-sex parent, grandchild and opposite-sex grandparent, elder and younger siblings of the opposite sex, and parents-in-law and children-in-law.

The pattern that exists here has much in common with that found among the Trio. Thus the closest relationship is between those of the same sex and age, and the most distant that between those of opposite sex and different age. As with the Trio the main exceptions to this rule result from marriageability and involve, as well as the spouse, the spouse's same-sex siblings and opposite-sex cross-cousins. When marriageability is present the relationship between those of the opposite sex is characterized by joking, in its absence by authority.

It is not possible to be definite about the influence of affinability because the ethnographer provides no information on the mother's brother–sister's children and father's sister–brother's children relationships. The relationship between parents-in-law and son-in-law and between father-in-law and daughter-in-law is one of restrained authority, but between mother-in-law and daughter-in-law the formality is said to be somewhat attenuated. This suggests that, with the exception of father-in-law–son-in-law, the relationship between affines of adjacent genea-logical levels does not diverge from the pattern that can be predicted on the basis of age and sex alone. Accordingly it seems safe to assume that affinability is not an important determinant of behavior among the Ye'cuana, whereas affinity does lead to some increased restraint, most markedly in the relationship between wife's father and daughter's husband.

A further point to note here is that there is no separate affinal term for a brother-in-law who is classified as a cross-cousin. The behavior between cross-cousins is of unrestrained joking, and in this the relationship is quite distinct from that between parents-in-law and children-in-law, for whom separate affinal terms do exist. Although this is a clear-cut case of different terminological usage being associated with varying behavioral practices, the Ye'cuana case may also be used to illustrate the opposite point, that members of the same category may be distinguished from one another on behavioral grounds. The Ye'cuana, as noted above, do not distinguish in address between opposite-sex siblings and opposite-sex cross-cousins, although the relationship between the former is described as one of restrained authority, and the latter as one of restrained joking. A similar point can be made with reference to full siblings and classificatory siblings of the same sex who, although terminologically equated, are behaviorally differentiated. Finally, in behavioral terms classificatory siblings and cross-cousins are associated although terminologically distinguished.

This suggests that an increase in genealogical distance among those of similar age results in greater freedom in the relationship and that the more formal pattern of relationships only applies among the more closely related. Given what else we know about the Ye'cuana, genealogical distance is almost certainly qualified by co-residence, both in the sense of creating kin of co-residents and strangers of non-residents. Thus it is arguable that the freedom that marks the relationship between the genealogically and residentially related (but not the most closely related) does not extend to the unrelated. There is sufficient evidence in the ethnography to indicate that the Ye'cuana suffer from the xenophobia typical of the region. On a particular point, Arvelo-Jimenez notes that in-marrying men present problems and encounter opposition because they threaten the ideal of group solidarity, which, among other ways, is expressed through settlement endogamy (1971:76). This fact indicates that the analytical distinction between related and unrelated affines has some significance in the Ye'cuana context.

At this point it is worth pausing briefly to look at the three cases so far considered. In numbers of purely affinal terms the Ye'cuana fall between the Trio and Pemon. For the Trio, the qualitative difference in attitudes and behaviors between related and unrelated affines coincides with the existence of a complete set of separate reference-only terms for unrelated affines. Among the Pemon no qualitative difference in the treatment of related and unrelated affines is recorded, and this occurs with a relationship terminology in which only two separate affinal terms exist and they are rarely used. In the Ye'cuana case, separate affinal terms exist only for parents- and children-in-law, and the conventional attitudes and behaviors between them are markedly different from those between brothers-in-law. In all these examples there is a coincidence between the presence or absence of separate affinal terms, of a behavioral distinction between related and unrelated affines, and of a qualitative difference in the relationship between kin from that between affines.

The Panare offer an example of a still different arrangement, for their relationship terminology contains a marked term for brother-in-law but no separate terms for parents-in-law and children-in-law. However, before examining the implications of this, we will start by looking at some of the other forms of conventional behaviors and attitudes that occur in Panare society.

Henley notes that of particular importance "in the organization of everyday life within the settlement . . . is the distinction between men and women" (1982: 134). Although it is normally a matter of male domination, Henley's account shows that the roles of men and women are complementary and that in certain contexts the expertise of the latter is accepted. Of particular interest is the account of the relationship between those who may marry: "In everyday life a man never addresses a potential spouse: to do so . . . makes one feel ashamed" (1982:135), and it is only at dances, after a lot of beer has been drunk, that young men feel free to approach marriageable women.

Beside the relationship between potential spouses Henley does not treat of other categorical relationships, but extracts four that he identifies as important in binding the conjugal family to the wider society (1982:128–33). These are those between mother-in-law and son-in-law, mother and daughter, siblings, and brothers-in-law.

The term for brother-in-law, *tamun*, is the single separate affinal term in the Panare terminology, but it is different from the separate affinal terms so far discussed inasmuch as they have all been purely referential. Whereas *tamun* in reference refers only to the actual brother-in-law, in address it may be used for all cross-cousins. The "real" *tamun* relationship is described as being "one of the most highly valued in Panare society: *tamun* are on intimate terms with one another and are supposed to be *ayape*, 'generous,' to one another" (1979:157). At another point Henley refers to the closeness of *tamun* in those cases where they have grown up together, and are thus likely to be related residentially and genealogically before being linked through marriage. He contrasts this with the restraint between an in-marrying man and his wife's brothers, but claims that this arises from his being a stranger rather than from the affinal relationship itself (1982:131).

The relationship between mother-in-law and son-in-law centers on the obligation of the latter to provide the former with meat, at least during the initial period of marriage. After this it is the intimate relationship between a woman and her daughter that influences the continuation of uxorilocal residence. The bond between a woman and her daughter is described as being that much closer than that between a women and her son, although this in turn is closer than that between a man and his son.

The solidarity of groups of same-sex siblings results partly from membership in the same family of birth but also through co-residence throughout much of their lives. Henley describes the relationship between adult brothers and sisters as being "in no way marked by the restraint that normally characterizes relations between men and women of the same age" (1982:130). Although his remarks are slightly ambiguous, Henley also indicates that there is a degree of restraint between a man and his son-in-law, but only a shade more than that which normally exists between men of different ages (1982:131).

J.-P. Dumont draws a slightly different picture of Panare relationships. He places greater emphasis on the role of the father-in-law, to whom the daughter's husband owes a series of services.[4] Dumont also writes that "in general, . . . a Panare man is closer and friendlier with his wife and his father, and therefore more distant with his sister and his mother's brother" (1978:121). Underlying this claim, and helping to explain the causal "therefore," is Lévi-Strauss's atom of kinship and the configurations of conventional attitudes associated with it. Although there is no reason to doubt Dumont's characterization of these relationships, and they do not contradict Henley's account, the application of the atom of kinship in this region of bilateral societies is of questionable value (begging the question of its value elsewhere), and its use to predict the content of relationships risky. Otherwise Dumont's description of the nature of Panare relationships is so intertwined with his own involvement with them that it is difficult to use his information.

As we have noted in other contexts, Villalón's description is very similar to that of Dumont. She refers to the bride-service owed to the wife's father (1978:747) and describes the relationship as one of reserve. The mother's brother–sister's son relationship is also described as distant because of the affinability it contains. Age and sex differences are the basis for variations in conventional behaviors within the settlement, although these are modified by familiarity and solidarity within the closest circle of kin. On the other hand communication with outsiders is difficult, and such interactions tend to be formal and awkward (1978:768–9).

Although Dumont's and Villalón's accounts differ in certain respects from Henley's, the differences are matters of variation rather than contradiction. Age and sex emerge as the important factors in determining modes of conventional behavior, but affinity, affinability, and marriageability serve to modify these. There is general agreement between the three ethnographers concerning the reserve in the relationships between affines of different generations, but there is a problem relating to ego's own generation. In the previous chapter we noted that the term *tamun*, which Henley gives for brother-in-law, is not mentioned by either Dumont or Villalón. Henley stresses the importance of this relationship among the Colorado Panare and states that it is characterized by a quality of generosity (*ayape*). Given the centrality of the brother-in-law relationship in Henley's account, we might be surprised to find it unimportant elsewhere. However, Henley also sees the relationship between affines of different generations in less formal terms than that portrayed by the other two ethnographers. Likewise these last make no reference to the restraint between potential spouses that marks this relationship among the Colorado Panare. None of this is inconsistent with one of the arguments that we have been developing; that the presence of a distinct term for an affine will be paralleled by a marked content to the relationship. Among the other Panare on whom we have reports, the absence of distinct terms for affines may be mirrored by a corresponding lack of difference in forms of behavior between affines and affinables.

However, there is a related subject, on which Henley is silent but to which

Dumont (1976, 1977, 1978) and Villalón devote a fair amount of attention. This is the suffix *-can*, which denotes affinity and is added, as appropriate, to a proper name (of which the Panare have very few – six male and four female). There is also the term *mwecan*, which denotes a general category of in-laws, both affines and affinables. Dumont states that *-can* "connotes the idea of return, of reciprocity with an idea of positive value" (1976:87) so that it may have something in common with *ayape*. Both ethnographers see its employment as a means of manipulating relationships, and Villalón (1978:767–8) sees it as a linguistic device for coping with the ambiguity fundamental to affinity. Despite the attention paid to the particle, the full significance of it remains obscure. From what is known it seems that it marks relationships of affinity and affinability in which the emphasis is on valued, but balanced, reciprocity. At the same time, the use of *-can* with a proper name implies the absence of any genealogical or affinal relationship, and in turn this might be read as evidence for the presence of a distinction between related and unrelated affines. That such a distinction does occur among the Panare is witnessed by Henley when he indicates that it is strangeness and not affinity that produces restraint among brothers-in-law. Villalón goes further than this and notes an increasing formality and decreasing affection as one moves from the circle of one's closest kin, and this is particularly marked in dealings with outsiders. With a little more attention to the differences that occur, the Panare case would seem to offer the only example in the region in which internal variation might be studied.

As our last full case we will examine the Piaroa (see Kaplan 1975:85–6, 177–80). Once again sex and age are the basic factors in determining the content of relationships. Thus a person of a senior genealogical level (assuming genealogical level and age coincide) is respected, and restraint marks the content of the relationship between those of the opposite sex. The exceptions to this occur almost exclusively in ego's generation. Thus the relationship between same-sex siblings is described as being "overtly intimate in nature," whereas that between brother and sister involves the "most rigorous restraint," more even than that between those of different generation and sex. On the other hand, the relationship between husband and wife is described as intimate and that between opposite-sex cross-cousins as one of familiarity, so that marriageability here overrides sex difference. The relationship between same-sex cross-cousins or brothers-in-law is one of distance and is marked by tenseness, formality, and a lack of joking. This last statement requires some qualification; Kaplan says that the conventional attitudes and behaviors hold only within the circle of close kin (*tük'u chawaruwang*) and that more distant classificatory cross-cousins will be on easy terms unless they become brothers-in-law. In brief, among related cross-cousins affinability overrides similarity of age but does not among the unrelated.

The distinction between kin and affinables that influences, even inverts, the content of relationships at ego's level has less effect on that between those of adjacent generations. The conventional behavior between a Piaroa and his father is identical to that between him and his mother's brother, or that between these two and that between a man and his father-in-law. However, this last statement is not true when strangers are involved, and the behavior between unrelated affines is characterized by more pronounced formality, restraint, and even avoidance. The Kaplans have recently stressed this point and with reference to the "polluting dangers of the stranger" have written that "to marry a stranger, a person distant from oneself geographically or genealogically, is to enter into a very dangerous relationship" (in press:68). The related/unrelated distinction plays an important role in the ordering of Piaroa affinal relationships.

Finally, on the question of the connection between the form of the relationship terminology and the content of the relationships, Kaplan herself notes that it is the brother-in-law relationship that cannot be disguised by the system of affinal teknonyms, and it is likewise the relationship, even when the participants are closely related, that is marked by affinal restraint and tension.

The five cases dealt with at some length are those from the region for which the ethnography on the topics concerned is full enough for a proper picture, even if obscure in some areas, to emerge. There is no reason to believe that these examples are exceptional in their broad lineaments, and the less complete information that exists for other groups (Macusi, Wapishiana, Waiwai, Waiyana, Aparaí, and others) indicates the same general picture, although with variations of the same order as those already identified. It is the major themes of the general picture that we must now attempt to summarize.

There are a number of interwoven strands here that have to be dealt with separately. In the first place, throughout the region, age and sex are the primary determinants of conventional behaviors and attitudes. Difference in sex and difference of age result in increasing social distance. To these must be added the factors of affinability, affinity (the fulfilment of affinability), marriageability, and marriage (the realization of marriageability). The tendency here is for these factors to modify the conventions determined by age and sex. However, the degree of modification and its application vary widely, and not all qualities operate simultaneously nor in the same way. Furthermore, these aspects are crosscut by a distinction between related and unrelated, which is most obviously influential in the case of affines but also applies to distinguish a group of close consanguines among whom the conventions of the wider society do not necessarily apply. Taking these various factors into account, the following general pattern emerges.

The relationship between members of adjacent genealogical levels is modeled on the age and sex differences. Marriageability has an insignificant role to play in such relationships, but the influence of affinability is more marked. Where the latter exists (Pemon, Ye'cuana, and Panare) it acts to strengthen the already existing attitude (usually one of respect) based on the age and sex determinants. Where it does not occur (Trio, Piaroa), the behavior and attitudes toward consanguines who are affinable (e.g., a mother's brother) and those who are not are similar. Where endogamous marriage (i.e., those involved being co-residential consanguines) occurs, behavior and attitudes undergo little change, no more perhaps than some hardening, as a result of affinability being transformed into affinity. However, the change is rather more complete when unrelated rather than related individuals are involved. The relationship becomes more formal and distant, and in some cases (e.g., the Trio) it is recognized to be of a qualitatively different sort. Thus, for any given ego, social distance from a member of an adjacent genealogical level increases with sex difference, age gap, diminishing degree of relatedness (which, it will be recalled, contains both a genealogical and residential component), and affinability/affinity.

The situation with reference to ego's own genealogical level is more complex and varied. It might be said that the relationships that exist at this level almost represent a paradigmatic set, of which other relationships in the society are weaker representations. First, the elder/younger distinction between siblings allows the incorporation of age difference to occur within this one level, and the relationship between elder and younger siblings is similar to that between members of different generations. Second, difference of sex is also important; siblings of the same sex are observed to have strong affectionate ties and cooperate in many spheres of life. The relationship between brothers and sisters is characterized by the restraint generally found between members of the opposite sex, although when there is a high degree of relatedness this is tempered by affection and marked by the organic solidarity associated with the complementarity of sex roles.

The relationships between cross-cousins, affines, and spouses represent a more varied pattern, which defies any easy summary. In the case of male cross-cousins, among the Panare and the Ye'cuana the relationship is one of relative closeness, even familiarity and joking. Distance characterizes the relationship between Piaroa and Pemon cross-cousins, whereas the Trio attitude of respect between cross-cousins is achieved by their terminological removal to adjacent genealogical levels. Marriage brings no radical change to any of these relationships when those involved are closely related, although there tends to be a firming-up of the premarital form. Thus, the relationship between Panare brothers-in-law is even closer than it is between cross-cousins, and where the relationship was prior to marriage marked by restraint it becomes increasingly so. However, a radical change does take place in some societies when the individuals concerned are not closely related. Thus, among the Piaroa, the free and easy relationship with a nonresidential classificatory cross-cousin becomes one of avoidance if they become linked through marriage.

Familiarity and joking characterize the relationship of marriageability among the Piaroa, Ye'cuana, and Trio. Panare cross-cousins of the opposite sex avoid one another, and among the Pemon this relationship is described as being of "maximum social distance," although sharing "structural parallels with the husband/wife relationship" (Thomas 1978:75, 77). Following marriage, these joking or avoidance behaviors are replaced by the complementarity central to the economic partnership involved in marriage, and the relationship between husband and wife is marked more by affection than familiarity.

If we leave aside the husband–wife relationship, we can represent the other relationships from ego's own genealogical level diagrammatically as follows:

| | Brothers | Sisters | Same-sex cross-cousins | Opposite-sex cross-cousins |
|---|---|---|---|---|
| Panare | + | – | + + | – – |
| Pemon | + + | .+ | – | – – |
| Piaroa | + + | – | – – | + |
| Trio | + | – | – – | + + |
| Ye'cuana | – | – – | + + | + |

Here the four relationships in each society considered in detail are ranked from the socially closest (double plus) to the socially most distant (double minus). Although this way of comparing structures of behavior has its faults, not least among them being that the signs are only crude representations of complex relationships, some points of interest are brought out by the table.

The first observation is that there is no consistent internal patterning to these relationships, so that by knowing the nature of one relationship or two one can predict the others. In the Panare case, the major contrast is between same-sex relationships and opposite-sex relationships. Among the Pemon and the Ye'cuana the main contrast is between consanguinity and affinability. For the Piaroa and Trio, the contrast lies between brothers and male cross-cousins, with whom are associated respectively their wives.

The second important observation to make is that behavior and attitudes are not intrinsic to relationships of consanguinity and affinability. Social distance, restraint, and avoidance are not an inevitable feature of affinability, nor familiarity and joking of marriageability, as a comparison of the Pemon and Ye'cuana so clearly indicates. Indeed this raises questions about the nature of affinity that we must now consider.

## III

Thomas has written recently that "the suppression of the quality of being an affine is a principle that we should expect to find, in various guises, in many if not all Carib-speaking societies" (1978:79). There is clearly some truth in this claim, for we have just documented the fact that people throughout the region find, in varying degrees, affinity to be an uncomfortable relationship. Even so, the claim needs to be looked at a little closer.

The seminal works on this topic are those by Basso (1970, 1973, 1975) with reference to the Carib-speaking Kalapalo of the Upper Xingu. The Kalapalo case differs in some important respects from those under consideration here, but there are some useful lessons to be learned from it. Before anything else, it is necessary to point out that Basso's term "affinibility" does not mean the same as "affinability" as used in this work, although there is a semantic overlap. The differences in meaning will become clear in the following discussion, but a major one is that "affinibility" incorporates the notion of marriageability, whereas I have separated out the latter from affinability.

The Kalapalo avoid the use of affinal terms except in certain specific contexts, but it is doubtful whether this represents an attempt to suppress affinity, as a consideration of behavioral forms will indicate. For the Kalapalo "affinibility" increases with social distance, which runs along a continuum from members of the same household, of the same faction, of the same village group, to those who speak the same language. Thus the marriage preference is for distant rather than closely related spouses. Thus a mother's brother's daughter from a different village would be preferred over a similarly related woman of the same village. In behavioral terms the situation can be expressed thus: The expected relationship between kinsmen is that of *ifútisu* (roughly supportive reciprocity including respect and generosity). The degree of *ifútisu* wanes with increasing social distance, so that as *ifútisu* decreases affinibility increases. At the same time the mark of affinal relationships is *ifútisu ékugu*, or strong *ifútisu*, although this does not apply to the spouse's same-sex siblings, with whom the relationship is free of *ifútisu* and is characterized by joking. Basso also writes:

Kalapalo affines may or may not be kinsmen, and affinal categories can be thought of as "neutral" with respect to kinship as a cultural category of relationship. This means that the concept of affinity does not contrast with that of kinship, nor is it a sub-category of kinship. However, the Kalapalo conceive of affinity as a unique type of status relationship, different from all other sets of rights and duties statuses, and use the distinctive label *ifútisu ékugu* to refer to it. (1975:214)

It is not clear why Basso regards spouses and potential spouses as affines when she states that the behavior between them is quite different from that between affines, but this is rather unimportant in comparison with what can be learned from the Kalapalo case. Their marriage strategy is different from that of the Guiana societies with which we are dealing, and a reflection of this is the incompatibility of the *ifútisu* of kinsmen with the *ifútisu ékugu* of affines. Marriage with a close kinsman will involve a difficult readjustment of previously existing behaviors. A similar case to this is to be found in the Guiana region, among the Maroni River Caribs who disapprove of marriage with close relatives on the grounds that it entails the mixing of incompatible roles (Kloos 1971:134). As we have seen in other Guiana societies, marriage with closely related people is preferred because it is the way of escaping the unpleasantness and ambiguity that are associated with marriage with strangers. In other words, the Kalapalo prefer to marry people the Guiana people prefer to avoid. When the Guiana people follow their preference and marriage occurs between those closely related, affines are neither terminologically nor behaviorally distinguished from kinsmen. Accordingly, when consanguinity and affinity coincide, they are neither contrasted nor distinguished, just as Basso suggests. However, when they do not coincide, it is a quite distinct relationship that has little to do with kinship and more to do with geographical and social distance.

We may return at this point to Thomas's claim that a general feature of Carib societies is their tendency to suppress affinity. Although he takes his lead from Basso, there is little that she says that would indicate that the Kalapalo try to do this. Indeed, her comments quoted above show that for the Kalapalo affinity is a highly marked relationship. If we look closely at Thomas's argument, it is not obvious that even the Pemon material supports his position. In brief, his argument is that because there is no distinct term for opposite-sex cross-cousin, affinity is being suppressed, or in his words "the structure of the Pemon zero generation categories, by its omission of an 'opposite-sex cross-cousin/eligible spouse' category for both male and female speakers, has imposed a kind of limit to the degree of social distance that can be expressed in the categories" (1978:75).

There are difficulties with this claim. As we noted earlier in this chapter, the failure to make a terminological distinction does not necessarily mean a distinction is not recognized. In the Pemon case it quite clearly is, because they distinguish between marriageable and unmarriageable members of the category by reference to the parental generation. Nor is a case made for the relationship between potential spouses being affinal, and evidence from elsewhere (including the Kalapalo) demonstrates that the behavior between potential spouses, that of marriageability in my terms, is quite distinct from that pertaining between either affines or affinables. As a rider to this, we may also ask why the Pemon suppress this category rather than the more obviously affinal relationships, such as those between brothers-in-law, and between parents-in-law and children-in-law.

Even if the Pemon case does not support Thomas's argument as strongly as all that, there are other examples that do, although at the same time they suggest a rather different emphasis and one more in line with other features of the region's social organization. On the basis of this I would like to rephrase Thomas's proposition in different terms, and then consider whether the notion of affinity, as the term is generally understood, is applicable within the Guiana region.

Taking her lead from Basso's reference to the use of affinal teknonyms among the Kalapalo, Kaplan argues that

the most important function of the teknonym system is . . . the eventual transformation of all affinal categories but one to that of "kin" . . . that the teknonym system is above all a recognition of the *Itso'de* as a unit of cognates is made evident by the Piaroa use of their teknonyms and their discussion about them. Affinal relationships within the *Itso'de* are ephemeral from the standpoint of the local group as a whole; for ideologically, in its entirety, and in accordance with the *chuwaruwang* model of kinship, it is a cognatic kinship group not segmented by a notion of opposition between kin and in-laws. (1975:174)

A Piaroa applies these teknonyms to closely related affinables and to actual affines whether they are co-resident or not. Furthermore, the nomenclature may be manipulated with reference to more distant affinables so that when one is on good terms with them a teknonym is used but when wishing to express anger or disapproval the "affinable" category is employed.

The second example is the Waiwai, and we will now return to some features of their relationship terminology that earlier were left to one side. The Waiwai concept of *epeka* has been discussed in Chapter 4, but other features of it are described by Fock. It is the group that includes "the closest, blood-related individuals of the same generation. Epeka are children of the same mother or of the same father, plus parallel-cousins, that is to say, classificatory siblings. As a rule it is an epeka group of this kind that dominates the economic life of a village. Indirectly related persons like wayamnu can by mutual agreement pass over to an epeka status and become 'declared epeka'" (1963:194). In other words this means that ego and his brother's wife may agree to call each other brother and sister rather than *wayamnu*, or that ego and his sister's husband or wife's brother may become brothers.

This institution is interesting in a number of ways, but among other things it helps explain what appears to be a number of anomalies in the relationship terminology provided by Fock. For example, although the term *poimo* covers such specifications as male cross-cousins and brothers-in-law, these same genealogical specifications are also covered by the term *nono*, which also means elder brother and male parallel-cousins. Exactly the same phenomenon is found with the term *achi*, which covers the specifications sister and female parallel-cousins, but also brother's wife and wife's sister, who are a man's *wayamnu*. The relationship terminology reflects the practice of "declared *epeka*" by which means affinal relationships are turned into consanguineal ones, at least terminologically.

It would be possible to agree with Thomas and argue that these cases are examples of the suppression of affinity. However, I wish to rephrase this as an emphasis on consanguinity and co-residence. Although it might be claimed that these are simply two sides of the same coin, the difference in idiom is all important. It has been demonstrated that the Amerindians of the region conceive of their settlements as populated by bilateral kindreds, which are ideally endogamous. We have also documented the fact that when endogamy does occur, it is difficult to distinguish in behavioral terms between consanguines and affines and such marriages do not involve any internal restructuring of the community. Within the ideal settlement affinity does not exist,[5] and its absence is a further aspect of Amerindian conceptions about the composition of a community. The concern is with the stressing of consanguinity, not with the suppression of affinity, which is not seen to occur in the ideally constituted community. The relationship that we have been referring to as affinity is not the product of marriage alone, but arises from marriage that involves a stranger. We need to return to the literal Latin meaning of *affinis*, "on the border," in order to regain the spatial component that is the essential feature of Guianan affinity.

Throughout the region the pervasive model of social space is based on a

*Social relationships*

concentric dualism with us on the inside and them on the outside. This distinction forms a theme running through Part III of *Marriage among the Trio*, and there is now no lack of additional supporting evidence. The Ye'cuana's "attitude towards non-villagers is one of covert suspicion and distrust at its best" (Arvelo-Jimenez 1971:323). For the Panare "the independence of settlement groups is expressed in the generally negative opinions that the members of any given settlement group have for members of any and all others . . . The more distant a settlement, the more the Panare suspect its members of being *tincakeihkye* [violent] . . . and the more their chauvinistic attitude to outsiders shades into fear" (Henley 1979:219). We have recently quoted the Kaplans on the Piaroa's view about the "polluting dangers of the stranger." Morton (1979) has isolated the inside/outside opposition as a dominant motif in Waiwai mythology. Social space is structured in terms of inside : outside :: kindred : strangers :: familiar : unfamiliar :: security : danger. The ambiguity of the affine, the in-marrying stranger, has to be understood within this framework, for it derives from it. The in-marrying affine is located between categories; he is here but not of us. It is not so much the suppression of affinity as that of strangeness that is sought; the endogamous marriage creates no ambiguity. But strangeness is not an absolute but a relative quality; there are degrees of otherness. Likewise there is no fixed dichotomy between "us" and "them," but rather a sliding scale with the distinction being drawn according to context.

This is inevitable, for however much a Guiana community may wish to lead an isolated and self-contained existence from which otherness is excluded, in practice this is not possible except for brief periods. Despite the mechanisms that help maintain the fiction of an endogamous kindred, affinity, like the outside, keeps creeping in. To understand the implications of this for the community we must examine political relationships, which are the subject of the next chapter.

# 6

# Autonomy and dependency

The focus so far has been on the settlement as an isolated, independent, and self-sufficient unit, and this approach is in accordance with the Amerindian's own view of the nature of the community. In Part I of this chapter this assumption is maintained while we look at the political relationships and processes internal to the settlement. This examination reveals that the actual size and stability of a settlement are to a large measure dependent on the relationships that constitute it. However, in Part II we have to face the fact that settlements are by no means the self-sustaining communities that native ideology proposes, and communication between settlements is vital for survival. The nature of the interaction and the mechanisms involved in their promotion are considered there.

## I

It is safe to start from the position that the settlement is an autonomous unit. Although the relationship between settlements is the subject of the second part of the chapter, it may be said at the start that there is little evidence for the existence in the region within living memory of any form of supravillage organization. In the absence of any overarching, hierarchically ordered institution each settlement is master unto itself, and its internal political structure is safely studied in isolation.

The vital relationship is between the leader and his settlement. The two are intimately associated, and the latter depends for its existence on the survival of the former. This relationship often receives linguistic recognition: The settlement is referred to as a particular leader's place, or he is known as its founder or owner. At death his village is normally abandoned. However, it would be wrong to place too much emphasis on the settlement as either a geographical location or a physical entity. It is better thought of as a set of people living together in the same place. A settlement is above all a social phenomenon, and successful leadership derives from an ability to handle the social network that constitutes the settlement and the community. This requires the possession of certain competences; these will be reviewed briefly because they have a bearing on the size and stability of a village.

The following is a composite list of the qualities required of a leader. In practice they vary from one society to another throughout the region, with this one receiving more emphasis here, that one there. First, a leader is expected to lead from in front, by example and by initiating activities, and not by issuing orders from behind. Second, he must be competent in performing and organizing routine affairs and be able to make correct judgments in such matters as where to build a village or cut a field. Third, he must be able to talk well, whether it be strong speech in dealing with outsiders, persuasive speech when things have to be done, or diplomatic speech when a dispute has to be mediated. Fourth, he must be generous, whether this is a matter of distributing or redistributing food and drink within the village or in entertaining casual visitors or other villages at dances. Fifth, he must be knowledgeable, usually in ritual or shamanism but also in tradition.[1]

The one thing the leader cannot afford to be is authoritarian. The leader has no means by which to enforce his will on others, and given the low tolerance for coercion within the region and the readiness with which people migrate if they find the social atmosphere disagreeable, the leader who oversteps the mark may find the size of his village dwindling. This is equally likely to happen if he is judged to lack whichever of the above qualities are regarded as crucial.

To these general statements certain exceptions have to be made. First, the more closely related people are to the leader the more likely they are to forgive him his failures, and the less likely they are to see his actions as authoritarian. Second, the relationships between men and women and that between adults and children are to some degree authoritarian, and in both cases the former is in a position to tell the latter what to do.

These last points are of some importance in understanding the political implications of village composition. This can be illustrated by taking the archetypal situation in which a village leader has a number of daughters and in-marrying sons-in-law. I pointed out some time ago (Rivière 1974) that throughout the region it is the affinal relationships that are politically important because they contain the potential for expressing hierarchy. However, what I did not make clear was that the subordinate position of the young men practicing uxorilocal residence is not direct but results from the control that the father exercises over his daughters, or even over his daughters via his wife. The nature of this control that men exert over other men through women is the topic of the next chapter. It has been alluded to here because the size and stability of a settlement depend on the number and nature of the affinal relationships it contains.

It must be remembered that the village political arena is very small. The average village contains around thirty people, and the largest rarely exceed fifty. Conceptually the village is composed of an endogamous bilateral kindred, and in practice the members are usually closely related, particularly in the smaller villages, although the larger villages will contain a penumbra of people more distantly related to the core. It is from this network of close consanguines that forms the village core that the leader finds his most loyal following. The problematic relationship is with those to whom he is related purely affinally, in other words as an unrelated affine. We have seen in the last chapter how affinity is associated with strangers and dangers, and we add here competition, conflict, and divisiveness. It was argued toward the end of Chapter 2 that it is unlikely that ecological determinants alone account for the upper limit of village size throughout the region, although ecological factors are likely to play their part alongside others. It was stated there also that ecological factors will have little to say about the social composition of a village on condition that it permits the completion of necessary subsistence activities. The question now to be faced, and it is the central political question of the region, is why do settlements become unstable and fission once they reach a certain size?

First, there is a lack of any mechanisms for settling disputes. Such mechanisms that do exist are little more than those that are necessary to maintain harmony within the extended family. As a village grows in size, the high degree of relatedness[2] that characterizes the small, tightly knit village diminishes, and there will be an increasing number of people over whom the leader will be unable to exert his familial power. With a large village, it becomes increasingly difficult to maintain the fiction that the village residents constitute a group of solidary consanguines. It is inevitable that the larger the settlement the greater the chance of dispute and the less the chance of resolving it, and this state of affairs is often recognized by the Amerindians themselves. Thus the size to which a settlement grows results partly from the nature of its constituent relationships and partly from its leader's competence, especially as a mediator.[3] However, any community contains the seeds of its own dispersion.

Conflict is an unavoidable fact of life throughout the region because it is an integral part of native cosmologies. Human agency is central to the notions concerning sickness and death, and as the latter are inevitable so too is the conflict that arises in their train. Once again, the larger the village the greater the frequency of sickness and death, and the greater the possibility of suspicion falling on a co-resident. Thus there are not only few means for mediating disputes but there are mechanisms that actively encourage them. Unresolved disputes, because of the lack of tolerance for disharmony, lead to the fissioning of settlements or, better put, to a breakdown in social relationships. This is because notions about the causation of sickness and death include a social component. Sickness, for example, involves not merely the malfunctioning of the human organisms but also indicates some failure in social relationships. Accordingly the shaman as curer also has a legal role to play (see Butt 1965–6). Further to this, the shaman, whether or not he is also village leader, has a political function that parallels that of the secular leader. One of the latter's duties is to represent his village in its dealings with the visible outside world; it is the former's obligation to represent the village in its dealings with the invisible outside world.

Dissension is by no means the sole cause of population movement. As we saw in Chapter 2, the Amerindians themselves provide lots of sound reasons for moving from one place to another; to dance, to trade, to visit kin, to exploit a particular natural resource, and even because there is a shortage of game where they are. From these general statements we must turn to the ethnographic detail and identify more exactly the political aspects of settlement and population dynamics.

We have already quoted Arvelo-Jimenez's remark that village history is political history, and we may now add to that Kaplan's claim that all movements are the result of individual political decisions and are responses to the questions "Which of my kinsmen can give me most [ritual] protection?" or "Which can teach me the most?" (1975:117). This emphasis on political motivation among the Piaroa may be a concomitant feature of their overall political structure that, as we have had occasion to mention and to which we will return later, represents somewhat of an exception in the region. On the other hand, the Piaroa have much in common with others in the internal political organization of their settlements. It has been hypothesized that smaller villages will be characterized by a dominance of consanguineal relationships and that affinal relationships will become increasingly predominant in larger villages. The Piaroa demonstrate this perfectly. "It is not by chance that the proportion of siblings-in-law living together is much greater in the *Itso'de* with large memberships than in those with smaller ones. The brother-in-law relationship, more than any other among the Piaroa, is highly political in nature, and large *Itso'de* can be built only through its exploitation" (1975:109).

It is necessary to refine the evidence further because not all affinal relationships are the same. Kaplan argues that the pivotal relationship in large villages is the leader's marriage, and the important thing is how other relationships are built around it. Relative stability occurs when an *itso'de* is composed of a bilateral extended family in which sons and sons-in-law are equally present. Stability is achieved through political relationships that are vertical, that is, between different generations. On the other hand, the leader who builds up his village through horizontal links, that is, with brothers-in-law, is at greater risk, especially when these are mainly through his wife to her kinsmen. Kaplan's example of this, the *itso'de* of Sera, illustrates the point well. Sera was mainly related to members of the *itso'de* through his wife, and the relationships were severed by her death. The competition latent in the settlement came into the open and the village divided into three. What is interesting is that as a result of dispersion the number of sibling-in-law relationships dropped from 88 percent to 50 percent, but the upheaval had little impact either on the proportion of parents and married children living together or on the proportion of same-sex siblings living together. It might also be noted that the death of the leader of a settlement constituted by a bilateral kindred where political relationships are vertical may result in an abrupt change to an organization characterized by horizontal political relationships. This will have a bearing, not on whether the settlement is abandoned (a foregone conclusion), but on whether its inhabitants continue to live together elsewhere.

The message from the Piaroa material is that although affinity is the way of obtaining a political following and thus building up one's village, affinal relations are fragile, although some more than others, and contain the seed of their own dissolution.

The Pemon case supports this position, although at the same time it offers an interesting contrast because of the differing nature of the settlement pattern. Among the Pemon only about half the settlements contain more than one household, and single-household settlements tend to be composed of little more than a nuclear family. Even the multihousehold settlements are small, and the largest naturally occurring settlement contains only forty-one people. This settlement is headed by a widower, who has with him the sons and daughters of several marriages; his sister, whose husband resides elsewhere; and two of her daughters, who are married to his sons. There are also two other married sons residing patrilocally. The next-largest settlement, with thirty-nine inhabitants, is also centered on a polygynous male who has managed to keep a married son as well as two married daughters at home. The only other settlement that the ethnographer classes as large contains thirty-two people, and here the core of the village is a group of women spanning three generations to whom the leader, a widower, is related as son, brother, and mother's brother. The ethnographer draws attention to two points. First, that in the two cases involving widowers, the men had returned to live with their sisters, having previously resided uxorilocally. Second, and this applies to the two largest villages, polygyny emerges as a factor in village size. In combination, polygyny and a brother–sister relationship offer the possibility of forming a large and endogamous settlement (Thomas 1973:146–7). At the same time, Thomas points to certain limitations on settlement size. "Limitations of the number of affines which can be held in the settlement by the head of settlement mean that the maximum number of households in a naturally-occurring Pemon settlement is about six" (1973:164). Giving a slightly different slant to the same claim, he writes elsewhere: "The possibility of naturally occurring Pemon settlements of size larger than about 50–60 seems to be precluded by the inability to hold more than two or three affines of the generation below that of the head of settlement within the settlement with any degree of permanence" (1973:251).

However, in his recent monograph (1982), Thomas has contrasted the relative strength of the hold that parents-in-law exercise over sons-in-law with the weakness of the relationship between brothers-in-law. Thus he writes: "Once the senior (parents-in-law) generation is gone, the siblings regroup at the expense of own-generation affinal ties" (p. 89). Among the Pemon the hold that the father-in-law has over his son-in-law may be expressed in terms of the obligation of the latter to care for the former, but in practice the effect is the same as among the Piaroa, where it is a matter of ritual dependency of the younger on the older. Likewise the Pemon may not express the same dislike as the Piaroa for living with a brother-in-law, but the effect on village composition is the same. Fission occurs between same-generation affines. Nominally a wife giver is superior to a wife taker, but in the absence of any groups that stand in such a relationship, this will depend on the individuals involved. Usually, because of his seniority, a father-in-law is in a position to exert a superiority that a wife's brother normally will not have over his sister's husband. Even with sister-exchange marriage, the arrangement most ideally suited for maintaining the settlement intact, there remains the tendency to fission with the demise of the senior generation.

The cycle of settlement development is related to the cycle of family development, and the stage in the life cycle has political implications. The single-household nuclear-family settlement increases in size to an extended-family unit as the children marry and have children of their own. The size to which a settlement reaches depends on, among other things, the longevity of its head and his ability to control the members of the junior generation, in particular his daughters and through them their husbands.

The importance of the life cycle of settlements is given a more fundamental role in the accounts of both Ye'cuana and the Panare. Arvelo-Jimenez, as has been described already, identifies three stages in the life of a Ye'cuana settlement. The first is the incipient village, whose inhabitants form a single three-generation family of eight to twenty-seven people. The village in its growth stage is likely to contain two or more such units, and a mature village of forty people and over consists of what is referred to as a joint household (a bilateral kindred) together with other families. Once a village gets to this stage it begins to become unstable, and people start to leave to found new incipient settlements. The question of who moves away is not clearly stated, and although the ethnographer claims that fission takes place along predictable lines she never makes explicit what these are. However, some evidence as to their nature is to be found in her work.

It is only by birth that an individual achieves full membership in a village, although an adopted child succeeds almost as well. The membership of those who join a village by marriage or invitation is described as artificial, and that they hold a marginal position or second-class citizenship is clearly indicated by the following quotations (Arvelo-Jimenez 1971): "In-marrying men are not always accepted . . . gladly" (p. 75); "men who marry into another village create problems for that village" (p. 76); "there are problems of assimilating a foreigner into village life and satisfying the group ideal of internal solidarity" (p. 76); "an in-marrying individual might encounter opposition from one or more family groups within the recipient village" (p. 76); "out of all the recorded cases of artificial attachment to another village there are only three cases of individuals . . . whose attachment to highly solidary family groups was quite successful"

(p. 85). Against this, "a small group of close kinsmen may secede from a mature and over populated village as well, but it is not likely to do so, particularly if it constitutes part of the village core" (p. 67).

The implications of this seem quite clear. There is a village core to which people belong by birth or adoption, and a village fringe who have joined through marriage or invitation, although the latter would seem usually to involve the former because invitations to individuals to join a village are "always accompanied by the offer of a local girl in marriage" (1971:85). It is the in-marrying group or individual who is likely to form the most unstable segment of the village population and is thus the most likely to migrate in the event of conflict. The case studies supplied support this conclusion. It is not feasible to examine them all, but we may refer to the case of Candao, who is a central character in the ethnography. His relationship with the main residential core of the village of Tawayu'ña is slender. He has one daughter married into the core group but living virilocally and another who is divorced from a member of the core group. His wife is a matrilateral parallel-cousin of three of the core group members, but this relationship has never been close. The core group itself is basically composed of two sets of intermarried siblings whose children have also intermarried. They thus form a solidary group with which Candao's household has only tenuous links. Candao's household is predictably the least committed to staying and the most likely to move out.

To return to the developmental cycle of settlements, although it would be wrong to see it operating in too mechanistic a way, it is a model that throws some light on the political process. Arvelo-Jimenez claims that it is in the growth stage that villages are most stable. In the incipient stage the constituent units are not well enough cemented together to prevent fission, and in the mature stage the presence of outsiders, that is, noncore members, heightens the chance of fission. The actual size to which a village grows depends on the sort of factors already discussed, and to them must be added a demographic aspect. The settlement in the most stable condition is one that is maritally self-sufficient. However, the chances of achieving this are remote, and the maturing village is almost certain to have to incorporate outsiders who will have a destabilizing effect.

When we compare the Ye'cuana with the Pemon and the Piaroa, the most marked difference seems to be that the important political relationship is not that between individual affines but that between the village core group as a political entity and those who are not members of it. However, I would wish to argue that given the average size of Ye'cuana villages and their impermanence what happens in practice is not much different from elsewhere. The notion of the core groups seems to be that of the Ye'cuana themselves and fits with the prestige they claim to derive from membership in a core group with a long history; a feature of Ye'cuana society that it is important to know more about (see Arvelo-Jimenez 1971:366–9).

Turning now to the Panare, it will be remembered that Henley identified three ideal types of residential groups. These are a man with his wife (or wives) and children; a man with his wife (or wives), married daughters, sons-in-law, and unmarried children; and a core of married siblings or siblings-in-law, with some surviving members of the senior generation, and married and unmarried children. Although these groupings could form stages in a developmental cycle, in practice villages oscillate between any of the three ideal types. Henley is more interested in explaining why nuclear families live together at all than in examining the processes involved in village growth and decline. This is not surprising, for Henley claims that "even when judged by the standards of lowland South American societies, the Panare are remarkable for their almost total lack of any political institutions" (1979:210). However, we can turn to J.-P. Dumont's work to help fill in the picture. His account of the recent history and political maneuvering in Turiba Viejo provides an almost classic example of the role of affinity in settlement formation. To take a single example, we may refer to the career of Ramón Gallardo, whose sister Teresa had been married to the former leader of Turiba Viejo, Manuel Blanco. When Manuel died the links between Ramón and the rest of the village became tenuous, and he found himself suddenly at the margin rather than in the center of the core group. However, when in the following year his two daughters married he was able to set up his own settlement with himself and his sons-in-law as its core (1978:ch. 6, p. 128). This single, brief political history involves two of Henley's ideal residential types (it is doubtful whether the relationships internal to the nuclear family could ever be defined as political), and affinity is basic to both. In the first Ramón is marginalized by the severance of what was purely an affinal relationship, and in the second he creates the core of his own settlement through the marriage of his daughters. That the relationship between a man and his sons-in-law is political Dumont makes clear, but Henley regards the tendency of such men to continue uxorilocal residence after the period of bride-service is complete to be the result of the affective relationship between mother and daughter rather than any control over the girl exercised by the father. What does emerge from the Panare material is that, as elsewhere, affinity is the means by which political relationships are formed, but at the same time they form the weakest links in the political structure.

A similar state of affairs is found among the Waiyana, although the relevant information is poorer. Hurault traces the changes that occurred in the villages of Touanké and Massili between 1957 and 1964. In the former village the ties, other than affinal, between the two groups forming the settlement were very tenuous. When a dispute arose the marginal group moved out, leaving behind the two women who had married into the core group. In the other case, the village of Massili split into two, one faction cohering around the leader Massili and the other around Tipiti. The relationship between Massili and Tipiti is affinal, but its exact nature cannot be derived from the genealogical information given (1968: 33–8, 72–3).

The Trio follow the pattern so far described. Affinal relationships, but above all those among unrelated affines, are political relationships. The relationship between unrelated affinables is also seen as political, as evinced by the use of the term *pito* (see Rivière 1974). The use of affinity in the formation of settlements has once again to be contrasted with the fragility of the relationship. In-marrying affines have difficulty in incorporating themselves into their wife's community. The degree to which a particular individual succeeds in this can be gauged by the extent to which avoidance behavior is relaxed and the use of relationship terms increases. The association in Trio ideas between anger, silence, avoidance, and sorcery suggests that suspicion of sorcery tends to focus around in-marrying affines and marginal groups. I contended some years ago (1970:249) that "within the village setting there is no structural position that seems particularly prone to suspicion." I now wish to revise that claim, and I see that I reached that conclusion by accrediting too much influence to relationship categories and not enough to the relationship between insiders and outsiders. I would rewrite it today to say that looking from the center, from the core group, outward suspicion falls on marginal members of the community and accusations on those resident elsewhere. However, I would stick by my claim made in the same article that the Trio village is a single-cell political unit that cannot survive internal division and competition. I now claim that this is true of all societies in the region, and that everywhere the problematic political relationship concerns the immigrant whose links to the co-resident core are solely through marriage. The number of such ties is important, and this, among other reasons, is why marriage strategies in the region include replication as well as reciprocation.

The notion of the settlement as an autonomous political unit and that of the settlement constituted by an endogamous bilateral kindred are congruent, which, given that the political and the social are expressed through the same idiom, should occasion no surprise. At the same time both are founded on a fiction, and in practice the autonomy of the settlement is no more real than that of its social self-sufficiency. Despite any native claims to the contrary, no settlement, like no man, is an island, entire of itself. Regardless of whatever views to which they may subscribe, many Amerindians are fully aware of the dangers of isolation and the advantages of interacting with other communities. In fact there are numerous mechanisms that maintain communication between settlements. It is to the relationship between settlements that we now turn.

## II

The factors that help to break down the physical and social isolation of settlements can be listed under a few general headings. These are marriage, disputes, trade, and ritual. The institutionalized forms these take vary somewhat from one society to another.

The small size of the average settlement and even the largest means that no community will long remain demographically self-sufficient, in the sense that it will contain a correct proportion of people of the right sex, age, and relationship for everyone to find a spouse locally. This fact of itself assures a certain amount of movement between settlements and the presence in other settlements of kin. This last point is important since it is the existence of kin in another village that eases access to it and assures hospitality there. Perhaps one of the commonest reasons given when people travel is the desire to see kinsfolk. However, this social network tends to be geographically restricted, and, as we have seen, the number of kin an individual can expect to find outside neighboring villages diminishes rapidly. Even so the value of having kin married into strange villages is not lost on the Amerindians.

That disputes function to redistribute people in different settlements is equally obvious, although initially providing a less satisfactory channel of communication. It was pointed out in the first section of this chapter that certain cosmological ideas, in particular those relating to the causation of sickness and death, makes disputes inevitable. Furthermore, the low degree of tolerance for conflict gives rise to migration. Although it is possible that the segment of the population that leaves a village may found its own settlement, it is just as likely that it will ally itself with another, existing village. The reverse side of the coin of mobility as a political institution is the granting of political asylum. Indeed, political asylum is an aspect of the hospitality that is generally extended to travelers in the region, although it is often extended more through the fear of strangers and as a form of self-protection rather than through any charitable motives. In the absence of such conventional hospitality, travel in the region would be that much more difficult, and it can be seen more as a way in which contact between villages is mediated rather than as an institution that in itself induces interdependency.

Clearly, for the proper functioning of trade, hospitality, and other mediating institutions such as ceremonial dialogue are important. However, there is the question of how far trade itself is simply a means of maintaining contacts between settlements. In other words, how far is trade concerned with the exchange of genuinely scarce or otherwise unavailable goods, and to what extent is scarcity artificially created (consciously or unconsciously) to produce and sustain sociopolitical relationships?

Coppens (1971) refers to certain intratribal trading among the Ye'cuana as "economically superfluous" and likens it to marriage and kinship as a means of relating basically independent units. Butt Colson (1973), in dealing with trade between the Pemon Arecuna and the Akawaio, sees the important factor as the uneven distribution of natural resources throughout the area, which in turn allows different local groups to monopolize them and to develop skills in manufacturing items from them. Second, there is the prestige that comes from owning exotic rather than locally produced goods. Finally, there is the matter of Western manufactured goods, the availability of which must have had a tremendous impact on native trading practices and routes.

Thomas is less certain that specialization, and thus trade, arises solely from the

81

distribution of raw materials and claims that "the totality of specialization which does occur *cannot* be explained on this basis" (1973:168). He provides a number of examples of products of which the raw materials are available to both the Pemon and Ye'cuana and concludes that "regional differences in resources account minimally (only, in fact, in the case of clay bowls) for the intra- and intertribal patterns to product specialization. Pemon are as capable of producing canoes and graters as the Makiritare [i.e., Ye'cuana] are of producing hammocks and baby carriers. The materials for canoes and graters occur in the western portion of the Pemon tribal territory but are not exploited due to intertribal division of labour. This division is primarily a cultural fact" (1973:246). Although he declines to make any guesses about the origins of this fact, he does note that it has some historical depth because it was reported by Simpson in 1939.

Kaplan (1975) favors the scarce-resource argument to explain Piaroa trade, and Yde (1965) does likewise with reference to the Waiwai. However, the latter makes the revealing comment that in the past the Essequibo Waiwai obtained their bows from the Mapuera Waiwai because the suitable wood was not available in the former area. However, when the Mapuera Indians moved north to the Essequibo the right trees were found there (1965:247). This form of specialism and division of labor is found among the Trio subgroups, and it is difficult to relate it with any certainty to the lack of a particular raw material, even though it is the Trio's standard excuse for not making some particular object. However, given the right incentive the raw material is suddenly found to be available after all.[4]

It seems likely that trade results from a combination of a genuine and pretended lack either of raw material or a requisite manufacturing skill. The mechanisms involved when the lack is not genuine remain obscure but the overall effect is the same. Trading is one of the most important ways in which villages break down their isolation. Unlike marriage, trade is extensive, and takes place well beyond the intensive network of kinship. This is made possible by a system of formal trading partnerships. Thomas describes this partnership among the Pemon as "the only supra-kinship reciprocal relationship . . . which manifests any degree of permanence" (1973:211). His description of the relationship indicates that it is very similar to the Trio form of the same thing, even down to identical terms for the trading partners (*pawana*). Among both groups a feature of this trade is not simply the permanence of the partnerships, but the delayed nature of the exchange, for it seems usual, even required, for months and even years to go past before repayment is made.

Not all Indians have trading partners, and those that do are likely to be relatively senior because such trading calls for human and material resources that are not available to the less influential. However, neither in the Pemon nor the Trio case is such trading restricted to village leaders, as is the case among the Piaroa. There the village leader (*ruwang*) trades on behalf of his village, and it is only he who can make long-distance trading trips because the layman is unable to protect himself against the supernatural dangers that threaten any traveler in foreign territory (Kaplan 1975:27).

Perhaps in the past, but certainly not within the period of recent ethnography, has there been any report from the region of "violent" communication in the form of systematic raiding for human trophies. The accounts available indicate little more than sporadic raiding as acts of revenge for sorcery or the abduction of women. Nor is there much evidence from the area that villages ever combined under a single paramount chief during periods of hostility. A possible exception are the Waiyana, who are described in the eighteenth century as having a centralized military organization with a hierarchical chain of command (Tony 1843). Over one hundred years later the organization had disappeared almost entirely, although some memory of it appears to have remained (Coudreau 1893:111). The Waiyana case may be similar to that described by Kracke for the Kagwahiv (1978). He concludes that the Kagwahiv have two "ideologies" of leadership, both of which have some support within their traditions. The more hierarchical, authoritarian form derives from a tradition of war chiefs, whereas the more egalitarian leader whose sphere of influence is restricted to his own settlement finds support in a clearly enunciated system of norms and values. Furthermore, if the Waiyana, like the Kagwahiv, are the remnants of a once much larger population that fled from the main waterways following the conquest (and this is a possible history for any of the groups in the region), then perhaps some folk memory of a previous, more elaborate political organization has remained.

The only other group among which there exists any form of supravillage organization are the Piaroa, but in their case the basis of it is ritual rather than military relationships. So far in this discussion on the ways in which communication is maintained between settlements, the institutions described are directly and explicitly concerned with the demand for scarce resources, be they people or things. When we turn to ritual the situation is not so clear-cut.

Ritual institutions that engender communication between settlements exist in numerous and varied forms, but in every case the mechanism is one of creating ritual dependency of one party on another. In some cases this is equally true whether the parties are individuals or communities. The Ye'cuana case makes this point very clearly. Arvelo-Jimenez writes that although "everybody has the technical know-how for making a living, only a very few have the ritual know-how absolutely necessary for individual and social survival" (1971:48). She also states that the exchange of ritual services establishes communication between settlements. At the same time ritual knowledge is a kind of wealth that is unequally distributed among the population, and the ritually poor are dependent on the ritually wealthy because most everyday tasks require some ritual input for their proper completion. Those ritually wealthy, the ritual specialists, are able to move around freely between villages, are invited to come and perform rituals in other villages, and in turn attract visitors to their own villages. "Ritually wealthy people are a visible link among villages and among household groups within a community" (1971:201–02). However, unlike most activities, and particularly subsistence tasks, which are mainly performed communally, a large amount of ritual is private and individual. There are relatively few public ceremonies, and none apparently that needs the participation of outsiders. Although the Ye'cuana grudgingly accept the importance of maintaining communication between villages, at the same time they restrict it to individual contacts and thus have been able to retain their view of the settlement as independent and self-sufficient. Indeed Arvelo-Jimenez's argument is that the Ye'cuana's representation of settlements as autonomous and self-contained is in contradistinction to the ethnographer's perception of Ye'cuana society as an aggregate of interlinked and interdependent settlements.

The comparison of the Ye'cuana with the Piaroa is interesting because relationships between villages are part of the latter's social awareness. Among the Piaroa political power is closely allied to ritual knowledge, for within an *itso'fha* the *ruwang* are ranked in terms of their ritual prowess, and the *ruwang itso'fha* is the person with the most. A factor in an individual's choice of where to live is the power of the *ruwang itso'fha* and his ability to provide supernatural protection. Competition between different *ruwang* is in terms of ritual knowledge, but at the same time because no *ruwang*'s knowledge is complete all *ruwang* are dependent on one another. However, to achieve the status of *ruwang itso'fha* it is also necessary to give successfully the *sari*, a territory-wide ceremony that lasts from July to September to which all the people of the *itso'fha* are invited. One may assume from this that the would-be *ruwang itso'fha* requires to demonstrate the possession of more than just ritual knowledge because he must have the resources to sponsor such a prolonged event. On the other side of the coin, the *sari* must also function as a sort of election because it is through the willingness of others to participate in the ritual that the *ruwang itso'fha* receives recognition and is confirmed in his position. The relative ease with which a person or settlement can change allegiance means that the territoriality of the *itso'fha* is more apparent than real, and the influence of a particular *ruwang* will expand and contract according to this own ability and success.

The Panare represent a different picture again. The knowledgeable man, *i'yan*, has no particular political role, and there is no reason why a village leader should be *i'yan*. With the possible exception of his ability to ward off supernatural attack on his village, he has little in common with either his Piaroa or Ye'cuana counterpart. The use of ritual to overcome settlement isolation operates here in a different way, and the mechanism is associated with the male initiation rites. These consist of three major ceremonies spread over the dry season and require a large amount of extra work on the part of the host community. Stress is laid on the collective manner in which these tasks are performed, and this contrasts with the usual individual style of subsistence activities. The preparation of the ritual gear to be worn by the initiands may not be made by members of their own families, nor may family members participate in ritual events that directly involve the initiand. For the most important parts of the ceremony this is taken a step further, and no members of the initiand's settlement may participate. The ritual actions have to be performed by visiting outsiders (Henley 1979:224–33). The effect of these rules is that in turn the independence of the conjugal family and the settlement is broken down, and they become dependent on a wider social network for the proper initiation of young men.

Rituals that enforce contact by ensuring that the successful outcome depends on the active participation of outsiders are common in the region. Among the Waiyana, male initiation rites and another ritual called *pono* require the attendance of outsiders, although what their duties are exactly remains obscure (Coudreau 1893:176–9, 227–35; Hurault 1968:ch. 6). Among the Trio, guests and hosts have distinct but complementary roles to play in dance festivals, and to this one can add that the Trio claim that happiness may be achieved only in company with others; an individual with other individuals, a community with other communities (Rivière 1969a:256; 1981:5). Among the Waiwai, in the ritual completion of a new house it is to young men from neighboring villages that the task of placing the architecturally inessential center pole falls (Fock 1963:169; Yde 1965:153).

At the beginning of this chapter it was claimed that demographic and economic constraints alone would operate to reduce settlement isolation. Although this is clearly true, I now wish to argue that they are by no means the most effective mechanisms to produce this end. One reason for this is that there are at least temporary palliatives for the demands that arise from these factors. Relationships can be manipulated so that a previously nonmarriageable person becomes marriageable and temporary polyandry is not uncommon. The lack of a previously traded item may be overcome through the discovery of the appropriate raw material or the recall of a forgotten skill. This is not true in the case of Western manufactured items, and why, until now, this factor has been ignored. The introduction of metal goods, irreplaceable from the natural resources of the environment, undoubtedly had an enormous impact on the relationship between settlements. This is a point that will have to be kept in mind when we consider the problem of scarce resources and the political economy of the region in the next chapter.

Perhaps more effective than demography and economy as mechanisms for reducing isolation are the cosmologies and causal notions of the region. The conflict and ensuing migration that are the inevitable concomitant of native ideas maintain communication by the continuous redistribution of the population. As a mechanism it is effective because there is no way of stopping it or circumventing it, for it is embedded in a system of ideas and causes of which the Amerindian is unlikely to be more than dimly aware. That this is so can be seen in the fact that migration is an open denial of their cherished belief in the community as composed of an enduring group of solidary kin. These two contradictory facets of life find resolution in the ability of the community to reseal its boundaries behind the backs of the departed.

Much of what has just been written about cosmology and causation applies equally well to ritual, although in this case the drawback is a mirror image. The former give rise to internal conflict, which is resolved by migration. Thus movement out restores harmony within. On the other hand, ritual brings people (often expressing hostility) into the village and produces harmony within.

This chapter has concentrated firstly on the political relationships within villages and secondly on those between villages. It has attempted to show that despite all their claimed autonomy the relationships internal to a settlement are in a dialectical relationship with those between settlements. How and why this is so is the topic of the next chapter.

# 7

# The individual in society

Although in the last chapter we described the political relationships that exist both within a settlement and between settlements, we avoided the far more difficult question of the nature of politics in the region. It is often said that the societies of Lowland South America lack, or at the best have poorly developed, political institutions. Clastres has argued that no true political anthropology can evolve while we insist on defining other peoples' political structures in negative terms: what they have not got in comparison with us. However, in the same breath, Clastres goes on to deny that the economy of Lowland South American societies is a political economy (1977:168). His argument is that in primitive societies the economy is not autonomous but is embedded in sets of other relationships. Although I accept Clastres's characterization of the economy as embedded I cannot agree with the conclusion he draws from it that there is no political economy. In contrast to Clastres, one may cite Turner, who writes:

Gê and Bororo social structure appears . . . as a form of political economy based on social rather than material production and reproduction. . . . It is a political economy based upon the exploitation of young women and men actively engaged in producing the basic social units of human production . . . by older men (and to a lesser extent older women), who form a dominant 'class' by virtue of their control of the crucial means of production (in this case, the obligatory setting of the productive activity in question), the residential household. (1979:168)

Turner's remarks are not fully applicable to the Guiana region because of the differences in social organization that exist between the peoples of the respective regions. However, they do contain ideas that are worth pursuing, and these will be taken up later in this chapter and the next. First, and this is done in Part I, the nature of the political economy in Guiana is explored. This leads us in Part II to consider the relationship of the individual to society.

## I

Political economy is taken for present purposes in the rather conventional sense of referring to the ways in which, within a given society, the production and distribution of wealth are ordered. The first difficulty is in identifying the nature of wealth, and it is perhaps Clastres's failure to do this that led him to deny Amerindian societies a political economy. That what constitutes wealth is culturally defined should not present a problem, because even dictionary definitions accept this proposition (see, for example *Shorter Oxford English Dictionary*). It is further arguable that wealth, whether it refers to health or riches, is inevitably unevenly distributed. Because of this, wealth is at the same time both a scarce resource and a value. Political economy is concerned with the management and control of scarce resources, and the ability to do this generates value for the individual involved.

What constitutes wealth in Guiana? At a number of places so far we have referred to the school of thought that sees the supply of protein as the primary determinant in tropical forest social organization and the factor that accounts for a whole range of institutions from the settlement pattern to infanticide and raiding. As has been indicated, there are obstacles in the way of fully accepting this position, not least because the data are by no means conclusive and rather similar figures may be used to support opposing points of view. This suggests that what is needed is an improved interpretative framework and that we require more thought rather than more facts. It is not the intention here to try and provide such a framework, but rather to assess the status of protein as a scarce resource and value with which the political economy of the region is concerned.

There is no denying that meat, the product of hunting and fishing and the main source of protein in the region, is highly esteemed. It is also, in a certain sense, a scarce resource, or at least an unreliable one. There is always uncertainty about the outcome of hunting or fishing, and hunters return empty-handed often enough for this to be clear. It is also true that prestige accrues to the successful hunter, but it is not always clear what exactly constitutes the successful hunter. Unfortunately this is not a topic dealt with in the literature, so I shall have to fall back on my Trio material for the following discussion. The successful hunter is not just a man who regularly returns home with game, but one who brings back certain sorts of game. Game is differentially evaluated, and the degree of prestige afforded the hunter reflects this evaluation. There is more prestige attached to the successful pursuit of wild pig than there is to capturing an armadillo, which, as like as not, is dug out of its hole in the ground. The former requires more skill, and this is one obvious basis for judging the hunter's prowess. Then there is the question of the relative scarcity of different sorts of game; to continue the same example, the population density of small animals like armadillos tends to be higher than that of larger animals such as wild pigs. But for the Trio there is an additional point: This is a species' potential for getting fat, for fat meat is much more highly esteemed than lean meat. Game is not just undifferentiated protein, and differences in the relative shortage of various kinds of meat, the skill required in obtaining it, and the preferred tastes of a people are the means by which the relative merits of hunters are judged.

88

The classic explanation of the political advantage of the good hunter is that his greater supply of meat gives him better access to women than a less successful hunter.[1] With more than one wife a man has at his disposal a labor force that is able to produce a surplus of processed food, in particular manioc beer. It is through the distribution of beer at ceremonies that he hosts that the successful hunter builds up the following that makes him a leader. However, it is unwise to accept too readily this rather simple and mechanistic association between hunting prowess, polygyny, and leadership. Vickers (1975) has shown that the difference between the best and worst Siona-Secoya hunter is small and cannot be related to differential access to women. Second, the causal flow from a plurality of wives to leadership is not certain, and polygyny is often the reward rather than the cause of leadership. Among the Piaroa, a man gains no particular political advantage from polygyny (although to reach the top he still needs to control a labor force that will produce a ritual surplus), and his control over meat results, not from having hunted it, but from having the ritual knowledge by which to render it edible (Kaplan 1975:38–9).

Furthermore, it seems rare that a young man, unless he resides alone, is free to dispose of his catch as he wishes. Control over it falls to a parent-in-law or village leader, and it is he who derives from the redistribution of meat the political power inherent in such an act. Another possibility is that the cooked meat is served at collective meals, to which each production unit contributes. This has the effect of nullifying the accumulation of political influence through redistribution, and, interestingly enough, this pattern is exemplified by the Panare studied by Henley, who claims that they are exceptionally lacking in political institutions.

This does not mean that every hunter automatically loses control over his bag, for this will depend on his position in the social network that constitutes his political community. Likewise there is no suggestion that hunting prowess is not convertible into political influence, because it is clear that a successful hunter does attract followers, and they are the proof of leadership. However, the important point is that the production does not necessarily remain with the producer, and control over his produce can pass to another who thus reaps its value. Unfortunately this is not a topic to which ethnographers have devoted much attention; however, it is one of peculiar significance, for the implication is that control over the product is only of secondary importance, and what matters is control over the producer who happens also to be the means of production.

We will return to this almost immediately, but first there is one further aspect of the game supply that needs to be considered. This concerns the native view concerning the relative and absolute shortage of game. I have no evidence that the Trio regard game as ever being in short supply in an absolute sense. They are aware that the supply of game in a particular area fluctuates over time, and they are also perfectly conscious of the fact that one of the results of living in large settlements, as they do at present, is that game is scarce within a day's hunting radius (they may complain about this, but for them the advantages available in the large settlements outweigh this lack). They do not doubt that if one moves to another area, game is plentiful, and this view seems generally to hold across the region. It is true that hunting is hedged around with ritual practices, whether these are to improve or ensure the skill of the hunter or to maintain the supply of game. However, it cannot be argued that the existence of such rituals is necessarily a response to a shortage of game. The relationship between human society and the animal world is throughout the region far too complicated for hunting rituals to be understood in such simplistic terms as renewal rites. It may also be noted that the failure of a hunter is seen to result not from a shortage of game (which is anyhow the unusual rather than the usual state of affairs) but from some ritual oversight, such as contact with a menstruating woman, that has affected his proficiency.

Let us now turn back to the argument concerning control over the means of production. Henley has written of the Panare that "in the absence of any individual ownership of the means of production (other than tools), no individual depends on another for access to them" (1979:115). Henley is right insofar as he is referring to natural resources (land, game, etc.) and using the concept of ownership, but his approach is too narrow, and means of production must include labor, or rather human resources in general. Scarcity in the region is not of natural resources but of the labor with which to exploit them. It is people who are in short supply. This does not necessarily mean any or all people, and exactly what sort of people are seen as scarce varies from one group to the next. In general, and this follows from the argument in Chapter 5, there is a relative scarcity of safe, familiar people compared with dangerous strangers.

Some of these points have been made by Harner (1975) with reference to the Jívaro. He argues that there is competition among men for women who are the scarce means of production of prepared foodstuffs that men convert into power and prestige. At the same time, because of high adult-male mortality due to warfare, there tends to be a surplus of women, and polygynous households are common. In such households, male labor is scarcer than female labor, and thus men are able to exert influence and control over women. The Jívaro case, because of the frequency of polygynous households as a result of exceptional demographic conditions, cannot be used as a general model. However, the underlying idea that it is women who are the scarce means of production deserves further attention.

On this question it is also worth referring to certain comments by Lizot on the Yanomami. He writes: "Les biens matériels et les denrées alimentaires ne sont pas rares; les femmes, elles, le sont" (1978:107). He goes on to claim that "en réalité, les femmes sont le bien rare dans l'absolu."[2] This may be the case with the Yanomami, and this is not the place to become involved in the disputes about the imbalance of the sex ratio and its causes among the Yanoama. However, there is no need for there to be an absolute shortage of women for them to be regarded as being in short supply. Given the size and distribution of settlements, an Indian is likely to be aware of only a small number of women, among whom the choice will be limited by assorted social factors (age, relationship, residence, etc.) and the supply always threatened by death, and perhaps abduction.

This last point is illustrated by the Trio, among whom there is overall a balanced sex ratio, although from the point of view of any particular individual or community the supply of women appears very restricted. Another position is taken by the Piaroa, who see scarcity not as one of women in general but of women whose relationships may be transformed through marriage into politically valuable affinal links (J. Kaplan and M. Kaplan: personal communication). For as Kaplan has stated: "The foremost aim of the *ruwang* is to expand the membership of the residential unit to which he belongs" (1975:146). This theme is echoed by Arvelo-Jimenez when she writes that "the major issue that divides the Ye'cuana is the allocation and re-allocation of personnel" (1971:370). J.-P. Dumont refers to the Panare headmen as attracting and retaining people (1978:129), and similar terms, "incorporation" and "retention," are used by Morton in his analysis of the Waiwai material. This being so, it is no surprise that marriage, insofar as it is concerned with the allocation of individuals, is such an important institution throughout the region. The case is well put by Arvelo-Jimenez (1971:136):

It [marriage] implies the relocation of a member who might be wanted by more than one group of close relatives or by more than one village. Marriages, then, are not outside the field of forces that make up groups, realign them, fuse them or split them apart. Marriages are useful means of consolidating some groups at the expense of others, not ends in themselves.

Furthermore, sorcery accusations and associated notions concerning sickness and death support this argument because they reflect worries about the total or partial disablement of human resources, and it is the shaman's duty to ward off such threats.

If we may accept that the political economy of the region is concerned with the management of human resources, which are normally seen as scarce, a number of questions still remain. In the last chapter it was noted that a man's control over his son-in-law is mediated through the authority he has over his daughter. The strength of the control is dependent to a degree on the actual or assumed shortage of women. How far a man will tolerate the demands of his in-laws will reflect the ease with which he can obtain another wife if he gives up the one he has. Although little evidence can be mustered for it, an explanation of female infanticide at least as plausible as some others put forward follows on from this. A generation that limits the number of its female offspring is reinforcing the control it will be able to exercise over sons-in-law. However, the matter of infanticide is not germane to the present issue, which is the nature of the authority that a man has over his daughter. This problem is best approached by generalizing it into the question of the nature of the relationship between men and women.

Most ethnographers have pointed out that an adult man and woman form a

91

self-sufficient productive and reproductive unit. The division of labor is organized along sexual lines, and the activities of man and woman are complementary. However, this interdependence does not result in equality. The evidence indicates that women have a longer working week than men (Hurault 1965, Lizot 1978), but this fact is relatively unimportant compared with the nature of what the two sexes respectively do and what happens to their products. One may compare hunting, the main subsistence activity of men, with the agricultural work and food processing that occupy women. Hunting is periodic and its outcome uncertain, but its product is highly evaluated, and once processed by women can be turned to political advantage.

The salient feature of women's work is the amount of time spent in the preparation of various manioc-based products. The procedures involved have been described often enough, and it is often assumed that they are necessary to remove the prussic acid that forms in the root from the oxidation of cyanogenic glucosides. However, the prussic acid is highly volatile and could be removed by far simpler means than those employed throughout the region. It is not clear whether other gains result from the traditional Amerindian method, but the varying degrees of elaboration in the process do suggest that the procedures are not purely technical. This variation is quite marked, and one can compare the complexity of the procedure found among the Tukanoans of the Northwest Amazon (see C. Hugh-Jones 1979) with the simpler methods that are used in Guiana. Even within Guiana, the processing and products are not everywhere identical. The information from Guiana is not detailed enough to show whether differences in the processing of manioc correlate with variations in social organization. However, the rather sharper contrast between Guiana and the Northwest Amazon does offer some clues. In the latter area the length and complexity of manioc preparation are present in a patrilocal society where the solidary male group is contrasted with the disruptive influence of individual in-marrying women (Goldman 1963:150). In Guiana, the simpler process occurs in uxorilocal societies, in which the cooperative core of a settlement is composed of related women. The argument that I wish to make from this is that the elaboration of manioc preparation beyond what is technically necessary is one of the means by which men maintain their control over women. The degree of elaboration is greater where the control over women is more problematic. The need to process the genuinely poisonous manioc provides the basis for control because, through the cultural elaboration of the procedures beyond what is technically necessary, the major female subsistence activity is routinized. Furthermore, although women are controlled by their commitment to the endless, daily routine of manioc preparation, at the same time they are denied all but the nutritional value of their labor. It is men who alienate the finished products of female work and use them for ritual and political purposes – spheres of activity from which women are effectively excluded.[3] The apparent complementarity of male and female subsistence activities masks the inequality that exists between the sexes. Nor is it only through the division of labor that men exert control over women. The important values stressed in the initiation of girls are patience, submissiveness, and hard work, while beliefs about the contaminating quality of menstrual blood further limit the freedom of women.

In family and marital relationships, the authority derived from maleness that the head of the household exercises over the women is normally reinforced by age difference. It is the subordination of women, above all younger women, that allows a man a degree of control over his sons-in-law; in other words it permits an extension of the control over women to control over men. In addition, so influential is the authority of age that it can have the effect of reversing the normal relationship between the sexes. Thus it is that a woman is able to exert some direct control, as well as that mediated through her daughter, over a son-in-law.[4]

At this point we might rest our case that the political economy of the region is concerned with the management of the productive and reproductive capacities of individuals, men and women, but particularly of the latter, who are the region's scarce resource, but there are some further matters that require attention. For example, we have not yet considered what value is generated by the successful manipulation of human resources, both for the leader and his followers.

An answer to this point is contained in Arvelo-Jimenez's work when she writes of the Ye'cuana that

In a society with no inheritable, material property and hence no goods to capitalize on, the only wealth of an individual is (1) his membership in an autonomous social unit, i.e., a mature village; (2) his membership in a locally compact and numerically strong group of close relatives; and (3) his ritual skills. The acquisition of the latter type of wealth is unrelated to kinship. . . . Kinship is the key factor in the acquisition of the first two types of wealth. (1971:63–4)

In other words, the successful manipulation of human resources, their incorporation and retention in a community by its leader, generates wealth both for himself and his followers.[5] The more successful the leader, the more secure in their wealth of social relationships, quite specifically co-resident kin (as we have seen, a tautology), are his followers. However, there are limits to which the leader can generate value, that is, build up the size of his village, and I will argue below that this is because he is operating in a political economy of people not of goods. First, it is necessary to deal with the claim that ritual skills also represent wealth.

To some extent we have already covered some of the discussion on this point in the last chapter. We have noted that among the Ye'cuana relationships of dependency between both individuals and settlements result from the unequal distribution of ritual skills. However, Arvelo-Jimenez makes it quite clear that this form of wealth is quite distinct from the other two types, both based on kinship and co-residence. Indeed she makes the point that the possession of ritual skills is a means of achieving the other two forms of wealth. This is even clearer in the Piaroa case, also discussed in the last chapter. The *ruwang* compete with one

93

another for followers through claims to ritual knowledge, but the highest status, that of *ruwang itso'fha*, can only be achieved by sponsoring a large and lengthy feast. The ability to do this depends on control by the would-be *ruwang itso'fha* over the surplus production of a large enough labor force, both men and women, and not on the control over any natural or cultural resource. The Piaroa case appears to represent an incipient move away from a political economy of people and toward a political economy of goods, but this move is constrained by the fact that ritual skill is not in the final analysis wealth itself but the means by which wealth is generated.[6]

The limitation on the size to which a leader can build up and maintain his settlement is inherent in the nature of the political economy. A leader lacks any formal means of control other than his personal influence and competence, and these are under continuous assessment by his followers, who have their own freedom of action. Herein lies one of the difficulties facing a political economy that seeks to deal directly with the distribution of human resources. It is not dissimilar to the problem that Lévi-Strauss noted with reference to the exchange of women in marriage: "Woman could never become just a sign and nothing more, since even in a man's world she is still a person" (1969:496). In other words, people, unlike goods, have minds of their own and do and say things of their own volition. To take this further we must examine the place of the individual in Guiana society.

## II

In the last chapter we dealt with the settlement both in terms of its autonomy and of its dependence on other settlements. The individual can now be treated in a similar way. In Chapter 1 attention was drawn to the frequency with which ethnographers have characterized the members of these societies as individualistic. It is the nature of this individualism that is to be explored here, and a start will be made by looking at some of the restraints on individual freedom of action.

With the obvious exception of biological reproduction, there are virtually no tasks essential to individual survival that necessitate cooperation. However, this deficit is compensated for by cultural factors. We have already noted that the culturally determined division of labor requires the cooperative efforts of a man and a woman to achieve economic independence. The husband and wife provide this complementarity within the nuclear family. Although the evidence is patchy, there is enough to suggest that the members of this unit are also tied together through sharing in a common substance. This has been best described for the Akawaio, among whom the sharing of common substances accounts not only for couvade restrictions but similar curtailments of diet within the nuclear family at times of serious illness (Butt Colson 1975; 1976:432). She also reports this among the Macusi (1975; 1976:432), and Thomas records the presence of shared substance among Pemon kin (1982:69–72). The Trio entertain similar ideas, and it seems probable that the Waiwai do also. [See Menget (1979) for an account of such notions among the Carib-speaking Txicão of Central Brazil.] Thus within the nuclear family under certain circumstances restrictions are placed on individual freedom of action in the interests of its other members.

Although single nuclear families do form autonomous settlements, particularly in the savanna region, they are normally incorporated in villages composed of several such units. There are some clear-cut advantages both for the family and for its individual members in surrendering the freedom of being a self-contained production and consumption unit in order to live with others. Some of these are cultural pressures, such as the Panare insistence that at least two men are necessary for a routine hunt and not less than three for a hunt preceding a ritual (J.-P. Dumont 1978:72). Others, such as the security that derives from living in a village during periods of hostility, have a less artificial nature. Finally, whatever drawbacks there may be for the nuclear family in restricting its independence are more than offset by the advantages that arise from membership in a system of communal distribution. Although an individual hunter may in theory be self-sufficient, in practice he is unlikely to be successful every day. The distribution of meat throughout a community assures the nonproducer a share. Even if the total production of five hunters over a period of time is no greater than five times that of one hunter, the catch will be more evenly distributed from day to day.

The advantages that can be obtained from living with others can only be obtained if individuals are willing to give up some of their personal freedom. It is true that a man who is unwilling to share his game with other inhabitants of the settlement can move elsewhere, but wherever he goes if he wishes to live with others he will be faced with the same requirement. Of course, these remarks are broadly applicable to any social existence, but they deserve to be made here in order to stress that the people of Guiana are no freer from the general constraints of social life than anyone else. What then is the nature of the individualism that the ethnographers of the region have so often noted? I hesitate to see it as some sort of psychological characteristic, but instead propose that it is an attribute of the atomistic social systems that the individuals constitute.

Attention to aspects of this has been drawn in Chapter 2. For example, the lack of pressure on natural resources because of the low density of population finds its social expression in the absence of a sense of territoriality or landownership, which in turn permits the freedom of movement and high rate of mobility that characterize the region. However, there is more to it than this, as Seeger, da Matta, and Viveiros de Castro (1979) have pointed out recently. These authors claim that the use of such terms as "flexible," "fluid," and "open to individual manipulation" to describe Lowland Amerindian societies is wrong because the conceptual norm against which they are being judged is that of Africa and other ethnographic regions. They argue that South American fluidity may well be an illusion, and that the difference is that South American societies are structured in terms of symbolic idioms that relate to the construction of the individual and the

95

fabrication of the body rather than to the definition of groups and the transmission of goods, as elsewhere. Although fully accepting the force of their argument, I think they have overlooked a crucial point that accounts for the high degree of variability within Lowland South America itself. This is the extent to which the construction of the person and the fabrication of the body is bound up with the reproduction of social formations. Comparative examples from outside Guiana will make this point clear.

Both the Gê-speaking peoples and the Tukanoans have social structures that contain the mechanisms of their own reproduction. These arise from an interplay between society and the individual. It is through membership in social groups that the individual obtains his social persona, but at the same time the social groups depend for their perpetuation on recruiting members. Or, as I have expressed it slightly differently, "the social persona results from recruitment in certain groups which thus maintain themselves by the enrolment of individuals" (1980:537). It is extremely difficult to identify any similar process in Guiana, for the simple reason that there are no social groups that survive the lifetime of single individuals. This is true of the nuclear family, even if it does reproduce itself; beyond it, the only social group is formed by the settlement, which has no continuity because its existence depends on that of the headman, whose network of relationships constitutes it. As J.-P. Dumont remarks, "la mort du leader est la mort du group" (1977:51).[7] Social groupings are only visible if we stop time, but their illusory nature becomes apparent once the clock starts again. This view is confirmed by an inspection of the role of rites of passage within the region compared with elsewhere. It is through rites of passage that individuals are recruited into social formations and thus perpetuate society. For example, the reproduction of Tukanoan lineages does not depend on biological birth through women but the creation of social persons through initiation by men. Although within Guiana rites of passage receive different degrees of elaboration from one society to another, nowhere are they involved with the reproduction of social formations. At the most they act to help break down the isolation of settlements, but more often than not they are simply concerned to transfer the person from one social status or category to another and to assure a proper individual development.

Turner (1979:165) has claimed that the "matri-uxorilocal residence pattern of the Gê and Bororo . . . tends to generate units that are relatively smaller, genealogically shallower, but more stably and effectively integrated within that shallow depth, than the patri-virilocal pattern of many . . . lowland Amazonian groups." The reason he gives for this greater stability and integration under uxorilocal arrangements is basically the same as that advanced in the first part of this chapter to explain the nature of politics in the Guiana region. It is the more effective control of men over women allowed by uxorilocal residence than that of men over men required under virilocal residence. I agree entirely with Turner about the potentially more effective control over women that can be exercised with uxorilocality, but I disagree with him about his diagnosis of the situation under virilocal residence. However, this can wait to the next chapter, and for the moment it is more valuable to examine his argument about the short-term effectiveness and narrow range of the uxorilocal arrangement. It results, he states, from the lack of any mechanism for extending what are no more than intrafamily controls. Thus there is no means whereby the father-in-law–son-in-law relationship can be generalized to other contexts. Nor on the death of the father-in-law is there any mechanism by which the brothers-in-law may be kept together, and this is the moment when the Kayapó household tends to divide into new domestic units.

This is also true in Guiana. The political relationship that links a man to his wife's father, whether this is mediated by the wife/daughter or not, has no ramifications outside that relationship. If the marital union that brought the relationship into existence ceases, so does the political relationship; when the father-in-law dies so does the relationship. There is no continuing commitment because there is no other individual, let alone group, to whom the son-in-law owes allegiance. It is the case that if a group of brothers has married a group of sisters the community may survive socially, if not geographically, its leader's death. The likelihood of this happening if the sons-in-law are unrelated is far less because the various marriages entail links only with the father-in-law and not with one another.

This, however, is where the similarity between the Gê and the Guiana cases stops. The crucial difference is the social context in which the uxorilocal household is situated. Turner refers to Gê "communities as agglomerations of multiple households" (1979:165). What needs to be emphasized is that these households form a community because their members are also members of social formations (age-sets, moieties, etc.) that are community-wide and have an existence independent of any individual relationships. These social formations function to hold the households together to form a community.[8]

Guiana settlements and Kayapó households have much in common, both in terms of their composition and their structural position. However, the former are dispersed, and this is consistent with the absence of any social formations to hold them together. It is this failure to combine individual sets of dyadic relationships into any higher and more enduring form of organization that gives the Guiana societies their peculiar stamp in the Lowland South American context.

The argument can be taken further than this. Turner argues that uxorilocality both generates and is enforced by the overarching communal institutions of the Gê. In other words, there are social institutions by means of which control over human resources is mediated, and this would seem to account for the apparent adherence to postmarital residence rules among the Gê. In Guiana, control has to be exerted directly because there are no scarce resources or social institutions through which it can be exercised. Although settlement endogamy and uxorilocal residence are preferred arrangements, these practices only occur as a statistical trend. One of the reasons for this is that the control a man has over his daughter is

97

not qualitatively different from that which a man has over his wife. There is no sanction to stop a man from persuading his wife to leave home and live elsewhere other than his inability to do so in the face of the opposing pressures applied by her kin. If uxorilocal residence is the commonest practice, it is because it reflects the young son-in-law's relative disadvantage in the battle of persuasion. However, the father's control is never assured, and the variation in settlement composition is the outcome of innumerable individual negotiations. Society is no more than the aggregate of individually negotiated relationships, and accordingly societal and individual relationships remain at the same order of complexity. It is for this reason that the Guiana Indian appears so individualistic.

If this conclusion is right, then it leads to certain other conclusions – in particular, to the conclusion that no distinction can be made between the reproduction of society and the reproduction of the person. In other words, society is no more than an aggregate of the relationships that constitute it. These are the terms we have used to characterize the settlement, and this should occasion no surprise for there is, so to speak, no society outside the settlement. It is, of course, true, as has been made plain in earlier chapters and is so clearly expressed by Arvelo-Jimenez, that "despite the apparent separation of each community . . . cognatic ties, extended paternity, and the kindreds . . . connect each of the villages into a global system" (1971:378–9). Even so, at any moment for any Indian, the village is his world, and in some cases, such as the Ye'cuana, the microcosmic nature of the house reinforces this view. It is through the settlement that the Indian locates himself in space, both socially and geographically. This much is plain, but more problematic is how these societies locate themselves in time and thus deal with the question of social continuity. Once again, the easiest approach to this problem is to look elsewhere first.

As we have noted, among the Northern Gê, the reproduction of the individual (as a social being) and the reproduction of society (as sets of social formations) are aspects of the same process. The actual process involved has been termed by da Matta "substitution" to distinguish it from descent.[9] He writes: "Continuity among the Northern Gê is obtained through substitution. In these societies, a person assumes a social mask from another and substitutes for him jurally and ritually" (1979:127). Substitution, which involves the transfer of name sets, takes place between the living and does not require any depth of genealogical knowledge. Indeed, all that is required is the narrow time scale afforded by two adjacent generations.

A slightly different perspective is provided by the Tukanoan peoples. Despite the presence of patrilineages among these people, it is not descent that is the important notion in the perpetuation of Tukanoan society. The patrilineages do provide some sense of continuity insofar as they are seen receding through linear time back to a generative source. Through ritual initiates are brought into contact with and are adopted by this generative source, the founding ancestors. However, alongside the lineal system is a much shallower two-generational system that reveals itself through the recycling of names and souls from grandparents to grandchildren, these qualities having originated with the founding ancestors. Furthermore, even within the patrilineal ideology, the two-generational model asserts itself when the founding ancestors adopt the new generation as their sons. It is clear that the cyclic transmission of souls and names is a more effective way of guaranteeing social continuity and reproduction than is the lineal transmission of physical substances. Tukanoan societies exist in a narrow time scale. (See C. Hugh-Jones 1979:161–5; S. Hugh-Jones 1979:249.)

The ethnography from Guiana on this topic is poor, but there are enough indications for it to be certain that these societies also exist within a restricted time scale. Indeed, given the nature of their social organization it would be surprising to find a greater time span than in the cases just noted. Genealogical memory rarely goes back more than two generations, and many Indians are ignorant of the names of their closest kin in the preceding generation. Such devices as teknonymy, the reuse of names in alternate generations, and a very limited supply of names all assist to promote genealogical amnesia. The recycling of soul matter is a common theme in the region, if not always too explicitly stated, and Frikel (1971) has reported that the Kaxúyana see life and death as alternating forms of experience. The restriction on time span is further heightened by the emphasis that tends to be placed on ego's own generation. The importance of sets of siblings among the Waiwai has been referred to, and this phenomenon has been well described for the Pemon. Thomas writes: "Pemon society can be thought of not only as individuals and families perpetuating themselves but, more widely and more importantly, as sibling sets trying to recreate themselves down through the generations" (1982: 70). Later he makes the important point that siblingship in each generation, specifically the brother–sister relationship, reemerges as a marital relationship in the succeeding generation (1982:90). In other words, each generation creates in the next generation the potential for its own recreation. The most powerful institution that performs this function is not, as might first be thought, the nuclear family, which is the unit in which reproduction takes place, but the relationship terminology. It is this last that allows for the orderly perpetuation of social life.

However, there is more to it than this, for there does seem to be a sense in which time is embedded in and represented by space. This is not a new idea in Lowland South America, and the degree to which both Gê villages and Tukanoan malocas incorporate notions of time and space is well documented. J.-P. Dumont has claimed with reference to the Panare that the shaman is conceptually related to permanence and the headman to impermanence (1977:73) without, unfortunately, exploring the point further. Morton (1979) in his reworking of the Waiwai material has adopted the terms "continuous" and "discontinuous" to describe respectively the spirit and human worlds, and I would like to borrow these terms from him. Continuous time is not in any sense linear time, but rather is is just and always there, indistinguishable from the cosmos of which it forms a part.

*Individual and society in Guiana*

Continuous time is like space, but like space is not undifferentiated; it is broken up by discontinuities. Settlements are both geographical locations and historical episodes. Discontinuities are located in continuous time in the same way as settlements are dispersed throughout the forest.

This is a somewhat speculative suggestion about the relationship between time and space in Guiana, but it is consistent with the narrow time scale within which these rather amorphous societies exist. The settlement is not only formed by coordinates of time and space, but it is also constituted by a network of social relationships. In turn, social relationships are ordered by a system of classification that is self-perpetuating. It is a system that not only allocates people in this generation but ensures an appropriate reallocation in the next. It is the combination of these factors that gives meaning to the present and assurance of continuity. In the present there is proof of the past and promise of the future.

# 8

# Guiana society and the wider context

## I

This work started with an examination of the nature of the settlement in Guiana; its size, distribution, and duration. The choice of where to begin was partly dictated by the need to provide something concrete on which to build the description of social organization. In practice, it has not proved feasible to move far away from the settlement as representing one of the fundamental social units of the region. Despite the ephemerality of its existence and the fluidity of its membership, the settlement appears as a relatively stable unit in comparison with the families and individuals who form it at any one time. Indeed, it is membership in settlements that gives families and individuals their social credentials and access to the wealth of social relations. In studying the social composition of settlements our attention was drawn continuously to the equation between co-residence and kinship and the stated preference for settlement endogamy. These factors go hand in hand with a contrast between the security afforded by kin, co-residents, and insiders and the dangers represented by others, strangers, and outsiders. It is the role of the village leader to manage the network of relationships that constitutes his settlement, and his and the shaman's duty to represent it in dealings with the outside, visible or invisible. Politics, insofar as they deal with the practical arrangements of living, are concerned as much with the relationship between settlements as they are with internal governance. The institutions that act to maintain communication between settlements, and thus save them from the dangers of excessive isolation, do not threaten the autonomy of each settlement.

It is arguable that autonomy would be more threatened by the refusal to cooperate in traditional forms of communication, however artificial they may appear, than vice versa. However, at the same time, settlements are in competition with one another, and this competition is for the one unquestionable scarce resource in the region – human resources, or the productive and reproductive capacities of men and women, although particularly of the latter. This competition, although in any particular case the outcome of individual negotiations,

101

results in a recognizable pattern in which the influence of certain social rules and expectations can be traced. Finally, it has been argued that Guiana society exists within a narrow time scale, and the difference between a synchronic and diachronic view is not great. Both aspects are mirrored in the life of the settlement. At one moment it is autonomous, self-sufficient, and apparently perdurable; at another it disintegrates and the elements that formed it, families and individuals, disperse only to create a similar pattern with like elements elsewhere. Although not entirely apt, the image of the kaleidoscope is the one that comes to mind.

In Chapter 7, it was found that increasing reliance had to be placed on other culture areas within Lowland South America in order to provide further illumination of the Guiana case. The reason for this is that the very formlessness of Guiana social organization makes it difficult to grasp what is there, and the more accentuated forms found elsewhere give clues about what to look for. This implies the assumption that the societies of Lowland South America have things in common. Certainly I subscribe to such an assumption, although it is as yet too early to identify what exactly these things are. However, I would hypothesize that within Lowland South America there are a number of subcultures, each of which represents a particular variation on a basic theme. On how many such subcultures there are it is difficult to hazard a guess, and in this book I have depended for my contrasts on two, the Gê-speaking peoples of Central Brazil and the Tukanoan peoples of the Northwest Amazon. I would further suggest that within this mosaic of variants, the Guiana region may hold a special place by representing the Lowland culture in its simplest form. In other words, other subcultures are more elaborate forms of the Guiana pattern. One needs to take care here to stress that such a claim does not mean that the Guiana subculture is being proposed as the origin of the Lowland culture, that from which all others developed. The proposed relationship is one of logical possibilities, and the Guiana subculture, as it so happens, exhibits the simplest of such possibilities. Although it may be too early to do so, the rest of this chapter is taken up with some indicators about the direction in which a wider comparative study of Lowland South America might proceed.

In a review article of four books dealing with different parts of Lowland South America, Kaplan has argued that "underlying their very dissimilar social structures is a similar philosophy of society" (1981:161). This philosophy is that "the universe exists, life exists, society exists, only insofar as there is contact and proper mixing among things that are different from one another" (p. 161). The apparent dissimilarity, Kaplan argues, arises from the fact that some societies, such as those of Guiana, attempt to hide the differences, whereas others, Gê and Tukanoan, readily reveal them. The danger for the Guiana societies of mixing unlike things is best evinced by a feature of the social organization that has already received considerable attention in the present work. "The most obvious masking device . . . is marriage with a close . . . relative within the house. The endogamous marriage . . . implies safety by keeping everyone home with close relatives and by making fuzzy the distinction between 'kin' and 'affines' " (p. 163). The necessity of, but at the same time danger of, mixing the inside and the outside is conveyed in Piaroa myth and, as Morton (1979) has shown, in Waiwai myth as well. The argument seems to hold equally well for the Tukanoans, whose mixing of differences is clearly and openly expressed in their marriage rules and practices. Recently Seeger (1981) has demonstrated how among the Gê-speaking Suya it is the interaction between society and nature that produces the cultural dynamism and the transformations that, in turn, create the individuals and social formations of their society.

In principle, I would agree with Kaplan's conclusion that "society as social rules – or as social structure – cannot be clearly distinguished from cosmological rules and cosmological structure" (1981:164). However, even if one accepts that social structure and cosmological structure are embedded in one another, and that in Lowland South America we have so many examples of one basic structure, the elementary structure of reciprocity in Kaplan's terms, there still remain some unanswered questions. If we can hold the philosophy steady, then it is still incumbent upon us to explain why the elementary structure of reciprocity gives rise to different social structures. It is this point that now receives closer attention.

## II

We can start by returning to a point left to one side in the preceding chapter. Turner, in a passage cited there, claims that a difference between uxorilocal and virilocal societies is that the former were better integrated in the short term because men's control over women is more effective than men's control over other men, as the latter arrangement requires. In practice, and as we have seen, the virilocal settlements exist in no greater time span than uxorilocal settlements, and it will be argued that the crucial difficulty faced by virilocal societies, at least in the South American tropical forest, is not so much the control of men over men as that of men over women. Some examples will make the point.

The examples I wish to take are to be found by moving due west across the northern part of the Amazon basin; from the Guiana region to the Yanoama to the Tukanoan peoples of the Northwest Amazon. It so happens that these cases form the basis of a comparative study conducted by Århem (1981), and this work deserves our attention.

Århem's own study is of the Tukanoan Makuna, and among them he identifies a form of social organization that he calls a "segmentary alliance system." The nature of this system is best left in his own words:

In a segmentary alliance system, the principles of unilineal descent and symmetric marriage alliance are both structurally determinant. Social groups are both descent-ordered and alliance-ordered; a combination of descent and alliance is responsible for both group cohesion and group perpetuity. The main formal features of the segmentary alliance system are, first, that it contains two or more, segmentary, lineal structures articulated by symmetric marriage alliance and, secondly, that allied lineal segments tend to be locally concentrated. In the particular Makuna form, residence groups are exclusively descent-ordered, while local segments above the level of the residence group are alliance-ordered. Over time, the alliance-ordered, local group segments and disperses in such a way that lineal and affinal distance is co-terminous with spatial distance. (1981:262)

It is the particular way in which descent and alliance are combined with a symmetric prescription that gives rise to this form of social organization. Other forms of social organization will occur with a two-line prescriptive terminology, depending on how the emphasis is placed on either the lineal or the alliance dimension. It is this proposition that Århem sets out to demonstrate with the help of Piaroa, Yanomamö, and Cubeo ethnography. He claims that with the Makuna inserted between the Yanomamö and the Cubeo these four groups form a continuum from the Piaroa, who place most emphasis on the alliance dimension and least on descent, to the Cubeo, who stress descent at the expense of alliance. At this point there are difficulties that Århem fails to overcome; in particular there is the difficulty of assessing the relative strength of alliance. He argues that "marriage exchange within low-level, spatial units indicates a stronger alliance system than marriage exchange between high-level units" (1981:276). In other words, the smaller the endogamous unit the greater the relative strength and efficacy of alliance. This is not obviously the case, and he threatens to topple in tautology when he continues: "Descent-ordered groups obviously indicate a strong descent system, and alliance-ordered groups a strong alliance system" (p. 276).

The measurement of the relative strength of alliance and descent is problematic, but there is no reason to assume that alliances between descent-ordered exogamous groups are less strong than alliances internal to a cognatic group. It is too often overlooked that exogamous descent groups are as much defined by their alliances with other similar groups as they are by descent. The importance of alliances is further increased by the presence of wife-exchange groups compared with the situation in which marriages are categorically ordered in the absence of any groups. It is true that Kaplan has argued that among the Piaroa "it is the alliance relationship – which in this case implies consanguinity – and not a principle of consanguinity alone, that is responsible for both group formation and group perpetuation" (1975:193), and Århem relies on this. But he also acknowledges that Kaplan appreciates that this is a fiction. Alliance may be responsible for the formation and cohesion of the group, but has no part to play in its perpetuation. Indeed, all Århem has done is document Kaplan's philosophy of reciprocity and show where the boundaries between the inside and the outside, as reflected in marriage practices, are variously drawn. This is useful and interesting in its own right, and his very rich ethnography on the Makuna shows that the size of the endogamous population in the Northwest Amazon is not all that dissimilar from that in Guiana.

In Guiana, whatever the ideal and fiction, most marriages do not take place within the settlement for sound demographic reasons. Most marriages occur within a cluster of villages that rarely receives terminological recognition, although it is identifiable by the density of the relationships and the nature of the interactions within it. Likewise, among the Makuna, the settlement (or residence group in Århem's terminology) is a member of a local group of such units "defined in terms of the network of agnatic kinship and marriage alliances" (Århem 1981:239). Within the local group, a Makuna will find most of his kin and affines. The observable differences between the two regions has less to do with the relative emphasis on alliance than with the social context within which the elementary structure of reciprocity operates. I shall refer to such operations in their social context as the mechanism of exchange.

Throughout the tropical forest, as distinct from Lowland South America which includes the Gê-speaking peoples, the allocation of people in marriage is a matter of central and lasting concern. More often than not this concern is focused on women rather than men. In Guiana there are no enduring social units involved in the exchange of women, and no mechanism other than the prescription embedded in the relationship terminology itself through which an exchange can take place. There is nothing to ensure that the giving of a woman in this generation will bring about a return in the next, and the only secure course of action is to effect an immediate exchange. Under such conditions, virilocal residence represents considerable risk, for when control over a woman is surrendered there is no mechanism that assures replacement. The alternative strategy is to maintain control over all human resources through endogamy or female resources through uxorilocal residence. However, because the actual means by which uxorilocal residence can be enforced are weak, strangers, that is to say potential affines, are regarded as a threat. The relationship between inside and outside, to which the fictional notion of a co-resident endogamous kindred and the denial of reciprocity are responses, is one of danger because the mechanisms of exchange are inadequate to mediate the opposition.

In contrast, we find in the Northwest Amazon more highly developed mechanisms of exchange. Here there are exchange units, residence groups defined by descent, that endure beyond a generation so that affinal ties formed in this generation can be carried over into the next. Furthermore, the reliance of these exchange units on one another within the local group and the shared interest in the women of the local group result in a system of generalized exchange (in Sahlins's sense of the words) that ensures each man a wife. Under such circumstances men can part with their women, confident that they will be replaced. Virilocal residence is a feasible arrangement. However, in the absence of a woman within the local group of generalized exchange, the matter becomes more problematic. Two strategies are possible. If a man has a woman to give away, then a direct exchange may be arranged with another local group. Whereas in theory this would seem to be an unproblematic solution, in practice there can be problems, for a man, in giving up control over the woman he gives away, cannot be assured of complete control over the woman he receives in her place. If a man has no woman to give in exchange, the second strategy to which he has to resort is capture. Within the fairly narrow social range of the local group the mechanism of exchange works well. Outside it, it is a matter either of immediate, balanced exchange or of abduction. The mechanisms of exchange are not capable of coping with delay nor of providing substitutes, such as bridewealth.

It is worth taking a brief look at the situation among the Yanoama. It is unwise to generalize because the variation among the different subgroups is considerable and deserves a separate study of its own.[1] For the present, it will be enough to say that, just as geographically the Yanoama lie between the Guiana peoples and the Northwest Amazon, so their social organizations show features similar to both regions. Some Yanoama subgroups, the Yanomam for example, have much in common with their Guiana neighbors, whereas others, the Yanomami central and the Sanumá, are characterized by the presence of shallow patrilineal descent groups. However, these last two groups differ in significant ways, and I wish to concentrate on them to make my point.[2]

Among both groups marriage is preferably settlement endogamous, but failing that the Sanumá practice uxorilocal residence and the Yanomami are virilocal, although uxorilocal residence is not unusual. At the same time, the level of violence in the form of raiding is higher among the Yanomami than the Sanumá. What I want to argue from this is that in Yanomami society control over women is not assured. The uxorilocal Sanumá are similar to the peoples of the Guiana region insofar as they retain by their postmarital residence practice direct control over their female resources. The Yanomami bear some similarities to the Tukanoan peoples, but it would appear that their shallow descent groups are less adequate as units of exchange. There are no safeguards for the man who gives a woman away voluntarily that she will be replaced; not unless, that is, he is strong enough to insist. Indeed, the Italian anthropologist Fabietti has concluded that:

le problème qui apparaît aux groupes yanomami est celui de faire face à un état de rareté des femmes que l'échange pacifique n'est que partiellement en mesure de résoudre. Les alliances, en effet, demeurent durables si le problème peut être résolu grâce à elles, mais elles sont au contraire fragiles si le manque de femmes est susceptible d'être résolu de façon plus radicale, surtout de la part des groupes les plus nombreux. Comme les alliances, la "guerre pour les femmes" peut donc être mise en rapport avec la "logique politique" si l'on admet que la violence est la moyen par lequel les Yanomami rétablissent l'équilibre et donc l'efficacité de leur système reproductif.[3] (1979:240)

In the various cases we have looked at, the structure of exchange as expressed through the relationship terminology is the same, but the mechanism of exchange differs in each case. The variable is the degree of control that each society exercises over its women. Further light can be thrown on this matter from a different perspective. Claude Meillassoux in his *Maidens, Meal and Money* (1981) voices dissatisfaction with traditional anthropological labels such as patriliny, matriliny, virilocal, uxorilocal, etc., and he proposes that attention should focus on two forms of mobility for pubescent adults. In the first, which he terms "gynecostatic," the women are immobile and men move to them, so that "the reproduction of the group rests entirely on the reproductive capacity of the women born within the group" (1981:24). In the second, which he calls "gynecomobile," men stay put and "women, exchanged on a reciprocal basis, do not procreate within their own community but in an allied community which recovers their progeny. Reproduction depends on the political capacities of the communities to negotiate an adequate number of women at all times" (pp. 24–5).

Gynecostatism is normally associated with matriliny, uxorilocality, and plant-ing agriculture (that is to say the cultivation of root crops, such as cassava, that normally need to be supplemented by other sources of food, in particular those obtained by hunting and fishing). Gynecomobility is usually found with patriliny, virilocality, and cereal agriculture. However, these correlations are not immutable.

The peoples of Guiana are clearly gynecostatic, and, except for the fact that they are cognatic rather than matrilineal, they accord well with the features expected of such societies. However, in one particular Meillassoux's argument goes astray as far as Guiana is concerned. He claims that if women are immobi-lized in their own communities, then a shortfall in women will threaten the continuity of a community that experiences it. This deficit cannot be rectified peacefully by bringing in women from outside because this will go against the gynecostatic principle on which society is organized. Meillassoux's answer is that the shortage has to be made good by violent means, and accordingly gynecostatic societies have "a permanent tendency to abduction and warfare" (1981:28). However, these are not common features of Guiana societies, despite the assumed or real scarcity of women that characterizes the region. Meillassoux's mistake is to have assumed that communities are isolated and bounded units, despite the necessity for men to move to other communities to find wives. As we have seen, not only do Guianan settlements continually disperse and reform, but there are also various institutionalized ways in which their isolation is checked. However, even if Meillassoux fails to appreciate this specific point (at least with reference to Guiana), he reaches another conclusion highly pertinent to the present argument. "Gynecostatism would thus represent a peaceful solution to matri-monial circulation . . . when political power is too weak to withstand the tensions and conflicts that reciprocal exchange of women would entail" (p. 28).

Bearing this in mind, we may turn to the Tukanoan case. These people are gynecomobile, patrilineal, and virilocal, and although not cereal cultivators they are an exception of the sort allowed for. However, what is clear is that there is a question hanging over "the political capacities of communities to negotiate an adequate number of women at all times," and this is perhaps more true of the Yanomami than the Tukanoans. Within the settlement or within the local group, where generalized reciprocity (once again in Sahlins's sense) is the rule, there is no problem, but beyond this social group the exchange of women must involve either balanced or negative reciprocity, because the groups lack the political capacity to negotiate any other forms of exchange. In other words, and in my terms, the mechanism of exchange only works within a restricted social range and in only rather limited terms. The mechanism is unable to assure the later return of a woman surrendered now when it is a matter of dealing with more distant groups. Exchange between such groups is either balanced and immediate or violent.

What then accounts for the different forms of social organization that are generated by Kaplan's "elementary structures of reciprocity"? The variation arises from the two components that make up the mechanism of exchange; one of these is a matter of distribution and the other of control. It is the interplay between these two components and between both of them and society that produces the variation. For example, in the Guiana case, distribution has been subordinated to control. The latter is achieved through the retention of women at home (i.e., uxorilocal residence), and short-term security is assured at the price of no lasting social formations. The reverse is also true, for it is the absence of social formations that can act as units of exchange that has stultified the development of the distributive component.[4]

Among the Yanomami there is an incipient development of the distributive component as is reflected in and caused by rather ill-defined exchange units, the so-called patrilineages. The weakness of these exchange units reveals itself in the uncertainty about control over women and an associated high level of competition for them. The Yanomami may represent the most inefficient of all mechanisms of exchange, because neither of the two components has the means of being properly effective. The Tukanoans suffer from some of the same problems, but on the whole the distributive element operates well within a given social range where the control component is satisfactorily fulfilled by the units of exchange. This is equally true when an immediate and balanced exchange can be made, but otherwise the situation is difficult. The problem of control reasserts itself because the mechanism of exchange is unable to allow for either substitution (i.e., bridewealth) or delay.

Finally, it is worth looking at the Gê, who seem to attach so little importance to marriage compared with tropical forest peoples. The explanation for this would seem to be that neither distribution nor control represents a problem because the communal institutions, which hold Gê households together in a single settlement, likewise operate the mechanism of exchange.[5] The paradox is that these communal institutions have their roots in an even more stringent retention of women than is found in Guiana, at the same time as they coordinate marriage exchanges. What seems to have happened is that the communal institutions have freed the Gê from a concern with transient individual relationships to focus on social reproduction.

This final chapter has been speculative in a number of ways, and it constitutes a limited attempt to broaden the lessons that the Guiana region has to teach. It indicates certain directions in which it might be worth exploring further. That being so, there is no conclusion to reach, for this end represents only a beginning.

# Notes

## 1. Peoples and approaches

1 This is a curious state of affairs since they are the groups of the region which have been longest in permanent contact with non-Amerindians. It is even odder when one realizes that access to them until relatively recently was very easy. Our ignorance of them is particularly unfortunate in the case of the Wapishiana, who are the largest population of Arawak speakers in the region, a linguistic group for which we have no detailed study.

2 One only has to think about the debate over the reasons for female infanticide among the Yąnomamö. It now appears that the rate of infanticide is very low, there is no discrimination against girls, and the sexual imbalance is the result of natural causes (Chagnon et al. 1979). If this had been known earlier on, it would have saved a lot of paper.

3 For example, the Maroni River Caribs, who "despite centuries of contact, change and near extinction" have maintained intact much of their traditional social structure (see Rivière 1974).

4 Colchester (1982:367–79) has computed that Sanumá (a Yanoama subgroup) cultivation with metal axes is three times more efficient than with stone axes.

5 A recent and preliminary attempt to provide a model of Carib social structure is that of Morales and Arvelo-Jimenez (1981). With the Pemon, Ye'cuana, and Karinya as examples, they set out to demonstrate that these three superficially different societies are constructed from similar units. The focus is on the residential unit, the economic unit, political systems, and intervillage relationships – topics central to this work.

## 2. The settlement pattern: size, duration, and distribution

1 It has been claimed that in the past the Trio had communal houses, which they abandoned for unstated reasons in favor of individual family houses (Bos 1973). A similar sort of claim has been made for the Waiyana (Hurault 1965:24). Although such an occurrence is quite possible, the evidence as it stands is unconvincing, and it is not worth discussing here since it has no bearing on the topic at hand.

2 It is questionable whether it is reasonable to regard as a village a settlement with only 2 inhabitants, but even if those settlements containing fewer than 5 people are eliminated the average village size only rises to 14.

3 Farabee states that his Diau could not be the same as the Drio Indians seen by Schomburgk in the same area in 1843, because the latter claimed that the Drio were tattooed all over the body whereas the Diau had tattoo lines only at the corners of their mouths (1924:252). However, it is clear from the vocabulary provided by Farabee that the Diau and Trio languages are the same.

110

4 The total of these figures, 59, does not agree with that of 69 which appears in Table 1 (p. 206).
5 The figures given by Fock for the Upper Essequibo differ slightly from those provided by Yde. Fock's figures are 40, 19, and 11 (1963:4). Given the normal mobility of these Indians, this discrepancy is not surprising.
6 Evans and Meggers have recently returned to their Essequibo material and attempted to produce a history of settlement movement in the area (1979). Although there is not room to deal with their analysis here, certain assumptions they make seriously weaken the validity of their conclusions.
7 There is a well-authenticated case of an Akuriyo woman with a young boy and girl surviving alone in the forest for several years. The Akuriyo are a Carib-speaking group of hunters and gatherers who wandered in the Trio-Waiyana area until settled in the late 1960s.
8 Thomas (1982:236) has recently gone further than this and written that the Pemon have a "social system which exists *to keep people at a reasonable distance* rather than bringing them 'together'" (italics in the original).
   It is unfortunate that Thomas's interesting monograph should have arrived too late for it to be possible to pay it in this study the attention it deserves.
9 One of the means by which this rotation may well be ordered is through shamanism. Both Fock (1963) and Reichel-Dolmatoff (1976) refer to the role of the shaman in regulating hunting among the Waiwai and Desana, respectively.

### 3. Village composition

1 De Barandiaran goes so far as to claim that "no se observa . . . mecanismo alguno eventual de cambio o de intercambio de mujeres entre los grupos mayores o entre las aldeas" (no possible mechanism of exchange or interchange of women between the largest groups or between villages is to be observed) (1966:52–3).
2 No gloss is given for the word *tapatakyen*, but the word does contain the syllables *pata*, which in many Carib languages translates as "place" or "village." One suspects that the word might be translated literally as "this village one just," meaning "just those of this village."
3 "The permanent residents of a community are called *tapatakien*, whereas kin are designated *piaka'*. However, as each residence group exhibits a certain degree of independence and endogamy, it happens that many of the *tapatakien* are recognised as *piaka'*."
4 In conversation, Paul Henley told me that he had met Marquito and had found him the most impressive Panare he knew. The account by Kracke (1979) of two styles of leadership is relevant here.
5 Except in citations I have adopted the most recent orthography, that from Kaplan and Kaplan, in press.
6 Thomas claims that there is no endogamous unit among the Pemon, by which he means a unit within which marriage must take place (1982:84). This is true throughout Guiana, and there is no group in which marriage must take place within a given unit. Endogamy in the region is expressed as a preference, ideal or fiction.
7 The Waiyana "do not consider the matrilineage and the patrilineage as two distinct groups."

### 4. The categories of social classification

1 A word for "family" in the restricted sense of the nuclear family is mainly absent from the languages of the Guiana peoples.

2 Arvelo-Jimenez states that a village that loses one of its members to another village feels that village to be in its debt (1971:76). However, given the impermanence of villages and the mobility of population, such a feeling of debt can be only short-lived and not a defining feature of the relationship between identifiable groups of any sort.

3 Wilbert in a recent unpublished paper has on the basis of some previously unused sources reached a similar conclusion. The earlier assumption that the Wapishiana previously had either an Hawaiian or an Eskimo terminology is no longer made.

4 However, Arvelo-Jimenez does mention (1971:329) a reference term for "the preferred category of close cross-cousins." The existence of such a term has recently been confirmed by Dieter Heinen. One might also note that Urbina, working among the Arekuna Pemon, has reported reference terms of opposite-sex cross-cousins for both a male and female ego (1979:109–10). The term he gives for female cross-cousin (man speaking) is *wirichí*, and for male cross-cousin (woman speaking) is *ukuraí*. These two words are very close to common Carib terms for "woman" and "man," respectively.

Although this information reduces the number of cases of terminologies without a term for the marriageable category, it does not deny the possibility of such an arrangement. Indeed, in the Pemon terminology collected by Thomas, there is another feature consistent with the absence of opposite-sex cross-cousin terms. This is that a man terminologically distinguishes his brothers' and male parallel-cousins' children from those of his sisters, female parallel-cousins and cross-cousins of both sexes. However, presumably when the female cross-cousin is married to a brother of ego, as she should be according to logic of the terminology, her children are classified as a brother's children.

It would appear that there is some awkwardness surrounding the use of such a term. This is certainly true for the Trio, among whom the word is rarely used in everyday conversation. Perhaps the best translation for such terms is "potential spouse" or "marriageable person," a category that includes the opposite-sex cross-cousins.

5 It is interesting to note that Fredlund and Dyke (1976:41) working with my Trio data computed that "given the age-sex structure of the population and known genealogical relationships, only about 16 percent of all marriages could have been made between preferred relatives if mating preferences were always followed."

6 The marriage of closely related members of the grandparent/grandchild levels is not entirely consistent with the claim that it is only distantly related members of these two levels who are of similar age who treat and address each other as cross-cousins.

## 5. Aspects of social relationships

1 This distinction is similar to but not identical with that proposed by L. Dumont (1957) between "genealogical" affines and "immediate" affines.

2 Entitled "The affinal triangle," Butt Colson's unpublished analysis of the long Pemon myth of Maichapue Pantoni documents this well, and in particular the trials and tribulations faced by the in-marrying son-in-law. One message of the myth is marry at home and avoid affinity.

3 This does not fit with Wilbert's (1958:54) claim, following Koch-Grünberg (1923), that spouses avoid one another. However, Wilbert does remark on the same page that the relationship between husband and wife is generally friendly.

4 The differences between Henley's and J.-P. Dumont's accounts have already been discussed. In this particular case it seems clear that the variable factor is the character of those concerned. Kracke (1979) has demonstrated well how the character of a headman can influence the nature of the relationships internal to his settlement.

5 Whereas the Shavante see heaven as a place without affines (Maybury-Lewis 1967:291),

the Guiana Indians appear to be trying to create such a heaven on earth. A rather similar idea seems to lie behind Kaplan's remark that "through endogamous marriage, the very notion of marriage exchange . . . has been erased" (1981:163).

## 6. Autonomy and dependency

1 Thomas (1982) has recently put forward the interesting argument that among the Pemon the powerlessness of politics derives from the fact that no man can simultaneously achieve expertise in all spheres necessary, because the requirements for each sphere are mutually exclusive. The roles he recognizes are those of leader, trader, shaman, and prophet. This is an interesting and original idea that deserves further attention. For the moment one might note that in the region prophets are more or less confined to the Kapon and Pemon, whereas it is not unusual to find elsewhere the roles of leader, shaman, and trader combined in the same person. Further research is required to reveal what the significant related differences in social structure are.

2 Chagnon (1975) also employs the notion "degree of relatedness," but his use differs from mine. His is based purely on the closeness of genealogical relationships, and because he takes this as measurable, his "degree" is quantifiable. I do not accept that relatedness is a purely genealogical phenomenon but regard it as entailing other factors such as the number of overlapping relationships and length of co-residence. Accordingly, I do not regard my degree of relatedness as quantifiable and use the expression merely in a descriptive manner. On a matter of conclusion, I would agree entirely with Chagnon that "as villages become larger, the average amount of relatedness among the members goes down" (1975:102–3), but this is purely a matter of common sense, not science.

3 Gillin noted this with reference to the Barama River Carib groups he studied when he stated that "there is a high correlation between the personal influence of the dominant character, his blood relationship with members of the group centering about him, and the spatial groupings of the households concerned" (1936:127).

4 A good example of this is given by Menget (1977:79–80) with reference to the Carib-speaking Txicão. Although they know how to make pottery, they prefer to steal it from their neighbors.

## 7. The individual in society

1 Morton (1979) sees the symbolic relationship between marriage and hunting among the Waiwai as inverted, whereas Århem (1981) sees it as direct among the Makuna. The different views are entirely consistent with the different postmarital residence practices.

2 "Material goods and foodstuffs are not in short supply; it is women who are the scarce resource" . . . "In fact, women are the absolute scarce resource."

3 A paper in which this argument is explored in detail is in draft form (see Rivière, n.d.).

4 Among the Tukanoan peoples, control over younger men by older men is exerted in a similar way to that by men over women. In this case it concerns the preparation of coca, an elaborate process in which the more routine and menial tasks fall to the young men. I am grateful to Christine and Stephen Hugh-Jones for pointing this out to me.

5 The truly successful leader will manage to arrange settlement-endogamous unions for his sons and attract sons-in-law to marry his daughters. This almost certainly accounts for the frequent references in the early literature to the practice of the leader's eldest son residing virilocally.

6 Both social and ritual competence as means through which to control people suffer from similar disadvantages; there is no objective assessment of them possible. The same act

or behavior may be judged by two people in entirely different lights depending on the relationship involved.

It is noticeable that differential access to Western manufactured goods rarely gives rise to political domination. An exception to this is the Sanumá dependency on the Ye'cuana for such items (see Ramos 1980, Colchester 1982). One possible reason for this occurring only intertribally is the difficulty of accumulating goods with traditional systems of distribution internal to a group. This, however, is not true everywhere in Amazonia; for the opposite situation, see A.-C. Taylor's (1981) account of the Achuar of Ecuador.

7 "The leader's death is the death of the group."

8 This functionalist interpretation is not uncommon. Lave writes of the Krikatí: "The age-set system integrated some ceremonial functions with some domestic ones. More important, it provided a strongly organized focus for men's activities which cut across domestic groups and made it nearly impossible for domestic group loyalties to serve as the basis for either communitywide factional disputes or, ultimately, the dispersion of the community" (1979:44).

Gross (1979) reaches a similar conclusion about Gê institutions starting from a rather different theoretical perspective.

9 I use the term "descent" for want of a better word, but I entirely agree with Murphy's (1979) strictures upon the employment of the notions of lineage and lineality with reference to Lowland South American societies.

## 8. Guiana society and the wider context

1 For an interesting study of the variation between the Sanumá and Yanomam, see Ramos and Albert (1977). However, I suspect their claim that "there are radically different structural principles at work" in the two groups (71).

2 For my brief account of the Yanoama I rely mainly on Lizot (1977), Ramos and Albert (1977), and K. I. Taylor (1977).

3 "The problem facing Yanomami groups is how to cope with a condition of the shortage of women that peaceful exchange can only partially resolve. Indeed alliances would last if the problem could be resolved through them, but on the contrary they are weak so the lack of women is liable to be solved in a more radical manner, especially by the largest groups. Like alliances, 'raiding for women' may thus be taken as part of the 'political logic' granting that violence is the means by which the Yanomami restore the equilibrium and thus the efficacy of their reproductive system."

4 This conclusion is vaguely reminiscent of Lévi-Strauss's comments on patrilateral cross-cousin marriage: "Marriage with the father's sister's daughter . . . never succeeds in creating anything but a precarious edifice made of juxtaposed materials, subject to no general plan, and its discrete texture is exposed to the same fragility as each of the little local structures of which ultimately it is composed" (1969:448–9).

5 There are variations among the Gê that deserve examination. For example, the Suya express a preference for sister-exchange marriages that are not found among the Northern Gê (Seeger 1981:129).

# Bibliography

Adams, Kathleen J. 1972. *The Barama River Caribs of Guyana restudied: forty years of cultural adaptation and population change.* Ph.D. thesis, Case Western Reserve University.
1979. Work opportunity and household organization among the Barama River Caribs of Guyana. *Anthropos* 74:219–22.
Århem, Kaj. 1981. *Makuna social organization. A study in descent, alliance and the formation of corporate groups in the North-Western Amazon.* Uppsala Studies in Cultural Anthropology, 4.
Arvelo-Jimenez, Nelly. 1971. *Political relations in a tribal society: a study of the Ye'cuana Indians of Venezuela.* Cornell University Latin American Program Dissertation Series, 31.
1973. The dynamics of the Ye'cuana ("Maquiritare") political system: stability and crises, International Work Group for Indigenous Affairs (Copenhagen), document 12.
Bakhuis, L. A. 1908. De 5de Wetenschappelijke Expeditie naar Binnenland van Suriname. *Tijdschrift van het Koninklijk Nederlandsch Aardrijkskundig Genootschap* 25:94–112.
Basso, Ellen B. 1970. Xingu Carib kinship terminology and marriage: another view. *Southwestern Journal of Anthropology* 26:402–16.
1973. *The Kalapalo Indians of Central Brazil.* New York: Holt, Rinehart and Winston.
1975. Kalapalo affinity: its cultural and social contexts. *American Ethnologist* 2:207–28.
Basso, Ellen B. (ed.) 1977. *Carib speaking Indians. Culture, society and language.* Anthropological Papers of the University of Arizona, 28.
Bos, G. 1973. Communale hutten bij de Trio Indianen. *Nieuwe West-Indische Gids* 49:143–62.
Butt, Audrey J. 1954. System of belief in relation to social structure and organization with reference to the Carib-speaking tribes of the Guianas. D.Phil. thesis, University of Oxford.
1965–6. The shaman's legal role. *Revista do Museu Paulista* 16 (new series); 151–86.
1970. Land use and social organization of Tropical Forest Peoples of the Guianas. In *Human ecology in the tropics* (ed. J. P. Garlick), 33–49. London: Pergamon Press.
Butt Colson, Audrey J. 1973. Inter-tribal trading in the Guiana Highlands. *Antropológica* 34.
1975. Birth customs of the Akawaio. In *Studies in Social Anthropology in memory of E. E. Evans-Pritchard by his former Oxford colleagues* (eds. J. Beattie & R. G. Lienhardt), 285–309. Oxford: Clarendon Press.
1976. Binary oppositions and the treatment of sickness among the Akawaio. In *Social*

# Bibliography

*Anthropology and Medicine* (ed. J. Loudon), 422–99 ASA Monograph 13. New York: Academic Press.

(with Cesáreo de Armellada), "The affinal triangle": some interrelationships between myth, social structure and personal anxiety among the Carib speakers of the Guianas. Unpub.

Chagnon, N. A. 1975. Genealogy, solidarity, and relatedness: limits to local group size and patterns of fissioning in an expanding population. *Yearbook of physical anthropology* 19:95–110.

Chagnon, N. A., M. V. Flinn, and T. F. Melancon. 1979. Sex-ratio variation among the Yąnomamö Indians. In *Evolutionary biology and human social behavior* (eds. N. A. Chagnon and W. Irons), 290–320. North Scituate, Mass.: Duxbury Press.

Clastres, Pierre. 1977. *Society against the state. The leader as servant and the human uses of power among the Indians of the Americas*. Oxford: Blackwells.

Colchester, M. E. M. 1982. The economy, ecology and ethnobiology of the Sanema Indians of South Venezuela. D.Phil. thesis, University of Oxford.

Coppens, W. 1971. Las relaciones comerciales de los Yekuana del Caura-Paragua. *Antropológica* 30:28–59.

Coudreau, Henri. 1893. *Chez nos indiens. Quatre années dans la Guyane Française (1887–1891)*. Paris: Libraire Hachette.

da Matta, Roberto. 1979. The Apinayé relationship system: terminology and ideology. In *Dialectical societies. The Gê and Bororo of Central Brazil* (ed. D. Maybury-Lewis), 81–127. Cambridge, Mass.: Harvard University Press.

de Barandiaran, Daniel. 1966. El habitado entre los Indios Yekuana. *Antropológica* 16.

de Goeje, C. H. 1908. Verslag der Toemoekhoemak-Expeditie. *Tijdschrift van het Koninklijk Nederlandsch Aardrijkskundig Genootschap* 25:943–1168.

1941. De Oayana-Indianen. *Bijdragen tot de taal-, land-en volkenkunde* 100:71–125.

Diniz, Edson Soares. 1968. A terminologia de parentesco dos Índios Wapitxâna. *Boletim do Museu Paraense Emílio Goeldi*, Antropologia 34.

1972. *Os Índios Makuxi do Roraima*. Coleção teses 9, Marília.

Dumont, Jean-Paul. 1976. *Under the rainbow. Nature and supernature among the Panare Indians*. Austin: University of Texas Press.

1977. Le sens de l'espace chez les Panare. In *Social time and social space in Lowland South American societies* (ed. J. O. Kaplan). *Actes du XLIIᵉ Congrès International des Américanistes*, vol. 2. Paris

1978. *The headman and I. Ambiguity and ambivalence in the fieldworking experience*. Austin: University of Texas Press.

Dumont, Louis. 1957. Hierarchy and marriage alliance in South Indian kinship. *Occasional Papers of the Royal Anthropological Institute* 12.

Evans, C., and B. Meggers. 1960. Archeological investigations in British Guiana. *Bulletin of the Bureau of American Ethnology* 177.

Fabietti, Ugo. 1979. De quoi les Indiens Yanomami ne rient pas. In *Le sauvage à la mode* (ed. J.-L. Amselle). Paris: Editions Le Sycomore.

Farabee, W. C. 1918. *The Central Arawaks*. University of Pennsylvania Museum, Anthropological Publications, 9.

1924. *The Central Caribs*. University of Pennsylvania Museum, Anthropological Publications, 10.

Fock, Niels. 1963. *Waiwai. Religion and society of an Amazonian Tribe*. National Museum of Denmark, Ethnographic Series, 8.

Fredlund, E. V., and B. Dyke. 1976. Measuring marriage preference. *Ethnology* 15:35–45.

Frikel, Protasio. 1971. A mitologia solar e a filosofia de vida dos Índios Kaxúyana. In

# Bibliography

*Estudos sôbre línguas e culturas indígenas*, 103–42. Edição Especial, Summer Institute of Linguistics, Brasília.

1973. *Os Tiriyó: seu sistema adaptativo*. Hanover: Kommissionsverlag Munstermann-Druck.

Frikel, Protasio, and R. Cortez. 1972. *Elementos demográficos do Alto Paru de Oeste*. Publicações Avulsas do Museu Goeldi, Belem, 19.

Gillin, John. 1936. *The Barama River Caribs of British Guiana*. Papers of the Peabody Museum of American Archaeology and Ethnology, Harvard University, vol. 14.

Goldman, Irving. 1963. *The Cubeo: Indians of the Northwest Amazon*. Illinois Studies in Anthropology 2.

Gross, Daniel R. 1979. A new approach to Central Brazilian social organizations. In *Brazil: anthropological perspectives* (eds. M. L. Margolis and W. E. Carter), 321–42. New York: Columbia University Press.

Hames, R. B. 1978. A behavioral account of the division of labour among the Ye'kwana Indians of Southern Venezuela. Ph.D. thesis, University of California, Santa Barbara.

1980. Game depletion and hunting zone rotation among the Ye'kwana and Yąnomamö of Amazonas, Venezuela. In *Working papers on South American Indians*, no. 2, studies in hunting and fishing in the neotropics. Bennington College.

Hames, R. B., and W. T. Vickers. 1982. Optimal diet breadth theory as a model to explain variability in Amazonia hunting. *American Ethnologist* 9:358–78.

Harner, M. J. 1975. Scarcity, the factors of production, and social evolution. In *Population, ecology and social evolution* (ed. S. Polgar), 123–38. The Hague: Mouton.

Harris, Marvin. 1979. The Yanomamö and the causes of war in band and village societies. In *Brazil: anthropological perspectives* (eds. M. L. Margolis and W. E. Carter), 121–32. New York: Columbia University Press.

Henley, Paul S. 1979. The internal social organization of the Panare of Venezuelan Guiana and their relations with the national society. Ph.D. thesis, University of Cambridge.

1982. *The Panare. Tradition and change on the Amazonian frontier.* New Haven: Yale University Press.

Herrmann, Lucila. 1946–7. A organização social dos Vapidiana do Território do Rio Branco. *Sociologia* 8:119–34, 203–15, 282–304; 9:54–84.

Holden, William H. 1938. Civilization and sudden death. *Natural History* 42:328–37.

Hugh-Jones, Christine. 1979. *From the Milk River. Spatial and temporal processes in Northwest Amazonia*. Cambridge: Cambridge University Press.

Hugh-Jones, Stephen. 1979. *The Palm and the Pleiades. Initiation and cosmology in Northwest Amazonia*. Cambridge: Cambridge University Press.

Hurault, Jean. 1961. Les Indiens Oayana. *Journal de la Société des Américanistes* 50:135–83.

1963. Les Indiens de Guyana Française. *Nieuwe West-Indische Gids* 42:81–186.

1965. *La vie matérielle des Noirs Réfugiés Boni et des Indiens Wayana du Haut-Maroni*. Paris: Office de la Recherche Scientifique et Technique Outre-Mer.

1968. *Les Indiens Wayana de la Guyane Française*. Paris: Office de la Recherche Scientifique et Technique Outre-Mer.

Im Thurn, Everard F. 1883. *Among the Indians of Guiana*. London: Kegan Paul, Trench.

Kaplan, Joanna O. 1975. *The Piaroa. A people of the Orinoco Basin*. Oxford: Clarendon Press.

1981. Review Article: Amazonian Anthropology. *Journal of Latin American Studies* 13:151–65.

Kaplan, J. O., and M. R. Kaplan. In press. Los Déa Ruwa. In *Los aborígenes de Venezuela*. Caracas: Fundación La Salle.

# Bibliography

Kloos, Peter. 1971. *The Maroni River Caribs of Surinam.* Assen: Van Gorcum.

Koch-Grünberg, Theodor. 1923. *Vom Roroima zum Orinoco*, vol. 3. Stuttgart: Strecker & Schröder.

Koehn, Sally S. 1975. Apalaí kinship and social behavior. *Arquivos de Anatomia e Antropologia* 1:79–108.

Kracke, Waud H. 1978. *Force and Persuasion: leadership in an Amazonian society.* Chicago: University of Chicago Press.

Lapointe, Jean. 1970. Residence pattern and Wayana social organization. Ph.D. thesis, Columbia University.

Lave, Jean. 1979. Cycles and trends in Krikatí naming practices. In *Dialectical societies. The Gê and Bororo of Central Brazil* (ed. D. Maybury-Lewis), 16–44. Cambridge, Mass.: Harvard University Press.

Layrisse, Miguel, and Johannes Wilbert. 1966. *Indian societies of Venezuela.* Instituto Caribe de Antropología y Sociología, Fundación La Salle, Caracas, monograph 13.

Lévi-Strauss, Claude. 1967. *The Scope of Anthropology.* London: Jonathan Cape.

1969. *The Elementary Structures of Kinship.* London: Eyre & Spottiswood.

Lizot, Jacques. 1977. Descendance et affinité chez les Yanõmami: antinomie et complémentarité. In *Social time and social space in Lowland South American societies* (ed. J. O. Kaplan), 55–70. *Actes du XLIIᵉ Congrès International des Américanistes*, vol. 2, Paris.

1978. Économie primitive et subsistance. *Libre* 78–4:69–113.

Maybury-Lewis, D. 1967. *Akwẽ-Shavante Society.* Oxford: Clarendon Press.

Meggers, B., and C. Evans. 1964. Genealogical and demographic information on the Wai Wai of British Guiana. In *Beiträge zur Völkerkunde Südamerikas. Völkerkundliche Abhandlungen* 1:199–207.

1979. An experimental reconstruction of Taruma village succession and some implications. In *Brazil: anthropological perspectives* (eds. M. L. Margolis and W. E. Carter), 39–60. New York: Columbia University Press.

Meillassoux, Claude. 1981. *Maidens, meal and money.* Cambridge: Cambridge University Press.

Menget, Patrick. 1977. Au nom des autres. Classification des relations sociales chez les Txicão du Haut-Xingu (Brésil). Thesis, Université de Paris X.

1979. Temps de naître, temps d'être: la couvade. In *La Fonction symbolique* (eds. M. Izard and P. Smith), 245–64. Paris: Gallimard.

Morales, F., and Arvelo-Jimenez, N. 1981. Hacia un modelo de estructura social Caribe. *América Indígena* 41:603–26.

Morton, John A. 1979. Conceptions of fertility and mortality among the Waiwai Indians of Southern Guiana. M. Litt. thesis, University of Oxford.

Murphy, Robert F. 1979. Lineage and lineality in Lowland South America. In *Brazil: Anthropological Perspectives* (eds. M. L. Margolis and W. E. Carter), 21–24. New York: Columbia University Press.

Myers, Iris. 1946. The Makushi of British Guiana – a study in culture contact. *Timehri* 27:16–38.

Ramos, Alcida R. 1980. *Hierarquia e simbiose. Relações intertribais no Brasil.* São Paulo: Editora Hucitec.

Ramos, Alcida R., and Bruce Albert. 1977. Yanoama descent and affinity: the Sanumá/ Yanomam contrast. In *Social time and social space in Lowland South American societies* (ed. J. O. Kaplan), 71–90. *Actes du XLIIᵉ Congrès International des Américanistes*, vol. 2, Paris.

Reichel-Dolmatoff, G. 1976. Cosmology as ecological analysis: a view from the rain forest. *Man* 11:307–18.

# Bibliography

Rivière, Peter. 1963. An ethnographic survey of the Indians on the divide of the Guianese and Amazonian River systems. B.Litt. thesis, University of Oxford.

1969a. *Marriage among the Trio*. Oxford: Clarendon Press.

1969b. Myth and material culture: some symbolic interrelations. In *Forms of Symbolic Action* (ed. R. F. Spencer), 151–66. Seattle: University of Washington Press.

1970. Factions and exclusions in two South American village systems. In *Witchcraft confessions and accusations* (ed. M. Douglas), 245–55. ASA monograph 9. London: Tavistock.

1971. The political structure of the Trio Indians as manifested in a system of ceremonial dialogue. In *The Translation of Culture* (ed. T. O. Beidelman), 293–311. London: Tavistock.

1974. Some problems in the comparative study of Carib societies. *Atti de XL Congresso Internazionale degli Americanisti*, vol. 2. Genoa: Tilgher. Also in *Carib-speaking Indians: Culture, society and language* (ed. E. B. Basso), 39–42. Anthropological papers of the University of Arizona, Tucson, no. 28, 1977.

1980. Review article: Dialectical societies. *Man* 15:533–40.

1981. The wages of sin is death: some aspects of evangelisation among the Trio Indians. *Journal of the Anthropological Society of Oxford* 12:1–13.

n.d. Of manioc, men, and women. Unpub.

Roth, W. E. 1915. An inquiry into the animism and folk-lore of the Guiana Indians. *30th Annual Report of the Bureau of American Ethnology, 1908–1909*, pp. 103–386.

1924. An introductory study of the arts, crafts, and customs of the Guiana Indians. *38th Annual Report of the Bureau of American Ethnology, 1916–17*, pp. 25–745.

1929. Additional studies of the arts, crafts, and customs of the Guiana Indians. *Bulletin of the Bureau of American Ethnology* 91.

Sausse, André. 1951. *Populations primitives du Maroni (Guyane Française)*. Paris: Institut Géographique National.

Schmidt, Lodewijk. 1942. *Verslag van drie Reizen naar de Bovenlandsche Indianen*. Department Landbouwproefstation in Suriname, bulletin 58.

Schomburgk, Robert H. 1841. Report of the third expedition into the interior of Guayana, comprising the journey to the sources of the Essequibo, to the Caruma Mountains, and to Fort Sao Joaquim, on the Rio Branco, in 1837–8. *Journal of the Royal Geographical Society* 10:159–190.

1841a. Journey from Fort Sao Joaquim, on the Rio Branco, to Roraima, and thence by the Rivers Parima and Merewari to Esmeralda, on the Orinoco, in 1838–39. *Journal of the Royal Geographical Society* 10:191–247.

1845. Journal of an expedition from Pirara to the Upper Corentyne, and from thence to Demerara. *Journal of the Royal Geographical Society* 15:1–104.

Seeger, Anthony. 1981. *Nature and society in Central Brazil. The Suya Indians of Mato Grosso*. Cambridge, Mass.: Harvard University Press.

Seeger, Anthony, Roberto da Matta, and E. B. Viveiros de Castro. 1979. A construção da pessoa nas sociedades indígenas Brasileiras. *Boletim do Museu Nacional*, Antropologia 32.

Simpson, George G. 1940. Los Indios Kamarakotos. *Revista de Fomento*, 3, Caracas.

Steward, Julian H. (ed.). 1946–50. Handbook of South American Indians. *Bulletin of the Bureau of American Ethnology* 143.

Taylor, Anne-Christine. 1981. God-wealth: the Achuar and the missions. In *Cultural transformations and ethnicity in modern Ecuador* (ed. N. E. Whitten), 647–76. Urbana: University of Illinois Press.

Taylor, Kenneth I. 1977. Raiding, dueling and descent group membership among the Sanumá. In *Social time and social space in Lowland South American societies* (ed.

J. O. Kaplan), 91–104. *Actes du XLII$^e$ Congrès International des Américanistes,* vol. 2, Paris.

Thomas, David J. 1973. Pemon demography, kinship, and trade. Ph.D. thesis, University of Michigan.

1978. Pemon zero generation terminology: social correlates. *Working papers on South American Indians,* no. 1, social correlates of kin terminology. Bennington College.

1982. *Order without government. The Society of the Pemon Indians of Venezuela.* Illinois Studies in Anthropology, 13.

Tony, Claude. 1843. Voyages dans l'intérieur du continent de la Guyane, chez les Indiens Roucoyens. *Nouvelles Annales des Voyages* 97:213–35.

Turner, Terence S. 1979. The Gê and Bororo societies as dialectical systems: a general model. In *Dialectical societies. The Gê and Bororo of Central Brazil* (ed. D. Maybury-Lewis), 147–78. Cambridge, Mass.: Harvard University Press.

Urbina, Luis. 1979. Adaptacion ecologico-cultural de los Pemon-Arekuna: el caso de Tuauken. M.Sc. thesis, Instituto Venezolano de Investigaciones Cientificas, Caracas.

Vickers, William T. 1975. Meat is meat: the Siona-Secoya and the hunting prowess-sexual reward hypothesis. *Latinamericanist* 11:1–5.

1980. An analysis of Amazonian hunting yields as a function of settlement age. *Working papers on South American Indians,* no. 2, studies of hunting and fishing in the neotropics. Bennington College.

Villalón, María E. 1977. Aspectos de la organización social y la terminología de parentesco E'ñapa (vulg. Panare). *Montalban* 6:739–73.

Wilbert, Johannes. 1958. Kinship and social organization of the Yekuána and Goajiro. *Southwestern Journal of Anthropology* 14:51–60.

1963. *Indios de la región Orinoco–Ventauri.* Instituto Caribe de Antropologiá y Sociología, Fundación La Salle, Caracas, monograph 8.

Unpub. Contributions to the study of Wapishana kinship.

Williams, James. 1932. Grammar notes and vocabulary of the language of the Makuchi Indians of Guiana. *Collection Internationale de Monographies Linguistiques,* vol. 8.

Yde, Jens. 1965. *Material culture of the Waiwai.* National Museum of Denmark, Ethnographic Series, 10.

# Index

121

# Index

endogamy, 4, 12, 31, 33, 34, 35, 36, 37, 38, 39, 40, 42, 49, 50, 51, 52, 61, 65, 71, 73, 76, 78, 80, 97, 102–3, 104–5, 111n6, 112–13n5, 113n5
  "prescriptive," 40, 49
Evans, C., 20, 37, 110
exchange, balanced, 106, 108
  generalized, 50, 105–6, 108
  mechanism of, 105–8
exogamy, 33, 37, 38, 49, 81, 104

Fabietti, U., 106
family
  extended, 11–12, 31, 32, 33, 37, 77
  nuclear, 11–12, 31, 32, 33, 38, 40, 42, 47, 79, 94, 95, 96, 111n1
Farabee, W., 18, 20, 37, 45, 110n3
Fock, N., 1, 20, 37, 38, 42, 47, 70, 85, 111n5, n9
Fredlund, E., 112n5
Frikel, P., 19, 99

Gê Indians, 41, 87, 96, 97, 98, 99, 102, 103, 105, 108–9, 114n5
Gillin, J., 1, 4, 22, 47, 113n3
Goldman, I., 92
Gross, D., 114n8
Guiana, as a culture area, 2–4
  as a subculture of the Lowland South American culture area, 14, 41, 102
  description of, 9–10
  geographical extension of, 2
  main cultural and social features of, 4, 10–14

Hames, R., 11, 28–9
Harner, M., 90
Harris, M., 26
headman, see leader
Henley, P., 22, 23, 32–3, 34, 42, 46, 48, 50, 51–2, 62, 63, 64, 71, 78, 79, 85, 89, 90, 111n4, 112n4
Herrmann, L., 37, 45
Holden, W., 20
houses, 11, 15, 98, 110n1
Hugh-Jones, C., 92, 99, 113n4
Hugh-Jones, S., 99, 113n4
Hurault, J., 11, 16, 17, 18, 24, 25, 29, 38, 79, 85, 92, 110n1

Im Thurn, E., 37
individualism, 4, 14, 94–100
infanticide, 88, 91, 110n2

Jívaro Indians, 90

Kagwahiv Indians, 83
Kalapalo Indians, 67–8, 69

Kaplan, J., 21, 34, 35, 40, 45, 48, 50, 51, 53, 64, 65, 69, 71, 75, 82, 83, 91, 102–3, 104, 108, 111n5, 112–13n5
Karinya Indians, 110n5
Kaxúyana Indians, 99
Kayapó Indians, see Gê Indians
kindred, 31, 32, 33, 34, 38, 39, 40, 70, 71, 73, 77, 80, 98
Kloos, P., 68
Koch-Grünberg, T., 21
Koehn, S., 4, 38, 45, 46, 47, 48
Kracke, W., 83, 111n4, 112n4
Krikatí Indians, see Gê Indians

Lapointe, J., 4, 17–18, 24, 29, 38, 47
Lave, J., 114n8
Layrisse, M., 23, 44
leader, 12–13, 27–8, 33, 58, 72–3, 74, 75, 82–3, 84, 89, 91, 93, 96, 99, 101, 113n1,n5
leadership, nature of, 12–13, 27, 72–3, 83, 89
Lévi-Strauss, C., 8, 63, 94, 114n4
Lizot, J., 90, 92, 114n2

Macusi Indians, 2, 5, 13, 16, 65, 94
  marriage among, 37
  postmarital residence among, 36–7
  relationship terminology of, 47–8
  settlement pattern of, 15, 24
  social composition of settlements, 36–7, 40
Makuna Indians, 103–5, 113n1
  see also Tukanoan Indians
Maroni River Carib Indians, 2, 48, 68, 110n3
marriage, 49–53, 65, 66, 80, 82, 91, 102, 103
  between genealogically related spouses, 51–2
  exchange, 50, 78, 105–6, 108
  practices, 14, 43, 50–3, 104
  prescriptive, 4, 12, 43, 47, 49, 53, 105
  rules, 14, 31, 49–50, 53
  see also polygyny
marriageability, 54, 59, 60, 62, 63, 65, 66, 67, 68, 69
matrilocality, see postmarital residence
Mawayenna Indians, 20
Maybury-Lewis, D., 112–13n5
Meggers, B., 20, 37, 111n6
Meillassoux, C., 107
Menget, P., 95, 113n4
migration, see movement of population
Morales, F., 110n5
Morton, J., 37–8, 71, 91, 99, 103, 113n1
movement of population, 24, 26, 27, 41, 50, 74, 75, 77, 78, 81, 84, 85–6, 95
Murphy, R., 114n5
Myers, I., 37

names, 4, 64, 99

# Index

outsiders, *see* strangers
ownership, 90, 95

Panare Indians, 2, 71, 90, 95, 111n4
  conventional attitudes among, 61–4, 65, 66, 67
  marriage among, 33, 50, 51–2, 79
  political relationships among, 78–9, 89, 91, 96, 99
  postmarital residence among, 34, 62, 79
  relationship terminology of, 42, 45, 46, 48, 61, 62
  ritual among, 84–5
  settlement pattern of, 15, 22–3, 25–6
  social composition of settlements, 32–4
patrilocality, *see* postmarital residence
Pemon Indians, 2, 4, 13, 81–2, 94, 99, 110n5
  conventional attitudes among, 57–9, 61, 65, 66, 67
  marriage among, 35, 36, 49, 50, 51, 69, 111n6, 112n4
  political relationships among, 76–7, 78, 113n1
  postmarital residence among, 35–6, 76
  relationship terminology of, 46–7, 48, 55, 57, 59, 61, 69, 112n4
  settlement pattern of, 15, 23–4, 27
  social composition of settlements, 35–6, 40
Piaroa Indians, 2, 10, 71, 82–3, 103, 104
  conventional attitudes among, 64–5, 66, 67
  marriage among, 34, 50, 51, 89
  political relationships among, 75–6, 77, 78, 84, 89, 91, 93
  postmarital residence among, 34–5
  relationship terminology of, 45, 48, 65, 69–70
  ritual among, 84, 89, 93–4
  settlement pattern of, 15, 21
  social composition of settlements, 34–5, 40, 69
political economy, 87–8, 91–4, 96–7, 101, 103, 105, 106–7
political relationships, 14, 72–86, 87, 97, 106, 107
polygyny, 36, 49, 76, 89, 90
postmarital residence, 34–5, 40
  uxorilocal, 4, 12, 31, 34, 35–6, 37, 38, 39, 40–1, 62, 73, 76, 77–8, 79, 92, 96–8, 103, 105, 106, 107, 108
  virilocal, 34, 35, 37, 38, 92, 96–7, 103, 105, 106, 107, 113n1
protein supply, 11, 26, 88
  *see also* ecological factors

raiding, 83, 88
  *see also* abduction
Ramos, A., 113–14n6, 114n2

reciprocation, *see* affinity, serial
reciprocity, elementary structure of, 103, 104, 108
Reichel-Dolmatoff, G., 111n9
relationship terminologies, 4, 12, 43–8, 53, 54, 55, 56, 61, 99, 100, 105, 106
  affinal terms in, 42, 43–4, 47–8, 56, 61
  and marriage, 49–53
replication, *see* affinity, serial
reproduction, social and individual, 95–6, 98–9, 103
resources, management of, *see* political economy
resources, scarce, people as, 90–1, 107
ritual, 12, 13, 73, 75, 77, 80, 83–6, 89, 90, 92, 93, 94, 96, 98, 113–14n6
specialists, *see* shaman
Rivière, P., 8, 19, 26, 35, 39, 40, 46, 53, 55, 56, 73, 80, 85, 96, 110n3, 113n3
Roth, W., 1

Sanumá Indians, *see* Yanoama Indians
Sausse, A., 17, 18
Schmidt, L., 17, 19
Schomburgk, R., 13, 19, 21, 110n3
Seeger, A., 95, 103, 114n5
settlements, 4, 11, 15
  as autonomous units, 12–13, 14, 72–80, 94, 101, 102
  fissioning of, *see* movement of population
  maximum and minimum size of, 25–7, 74, 79, 94
  nature of, 72, 98, 99–100
  pattern of, 11, 14, 15–29, 41, 73, 80–1, 88, 96, 101, 107
  relationship between, 12, 14, 80–6, 101, 107
  social composition of, 11, 12, 14, 15, 30–41, 52, 70, 80–1, 101
shaman, 12, 58, 74–5, 83–4, 91, 99, 101, 113n1
shamanism, 12, 73, 111n9
Shavante Indians, *see* Gê Indians
Simpson, G., 23, 82
Siona-Secoya Indians, 89
soul matter, 99
space, social, 70–1, 98, 99–100
Steward, J., 4
strangers, 65, 70, 71, 74, 77, 80, 81, 85, 101, 103, 105
Suya Indians, *see* Gê Indians

Taruma Indians, 19, 20
Taylor, A. -C., 113–14n6
Taylor, K., 114n2
Thomas, D., 4, 23, 27, 35, 36, 47, 48, 50, 51, 55, 57, 58, 59, 66, 67, 69, 70, 76, 81, 82, 94, 111n8,n6, 113n1
time, social, 96, 98, 99–100, 102

# Index

# CAMBRIDGE STUDIES IN SOCIAL ANTHROPOLOGY

*General Editor*: Jack Goody

125

\* Also available as a paperback.

127